the 20th Century
Broadway

W9-ADP-537

ISBN 0-634-02193-1

HAL•LEONARD® CORPORATION

7777 W. BLUEMOUND RD. P.O. BOX 13819 MILWAUKEE, WI 53213

Jefferson-Madison
Regional Library
Charlottesville, Virginia

Visit Hal Leonard Online at
www.halleonard.com

CONTENTS

1721 0681
A

ADELAIDE'S LAMENT
from GUYS AND DOLLS

By FRANK LOESSER

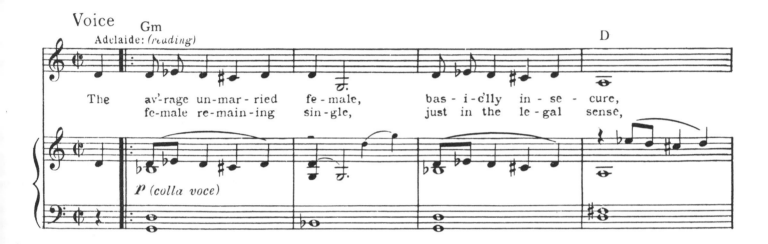

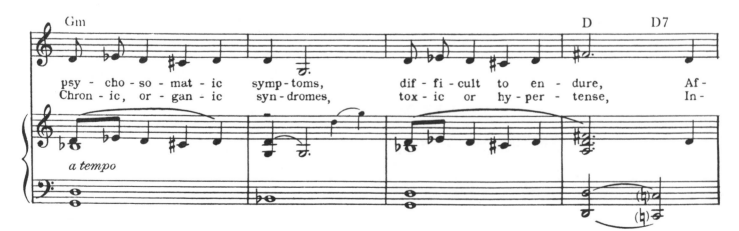

per - son _____ can de - vel - op La grippe. When they

get on the train for Ni - ag - 'ra and she can hear church bells chime, The com-

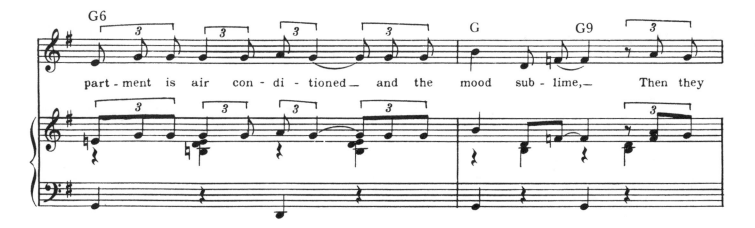

part - ment is air con - di - tioned ___ and the mood sub - lime, ___ Then they

get off at Sar - a - to - ga ___ for the four-teenth time, A per - son ___ can de - vel - op La

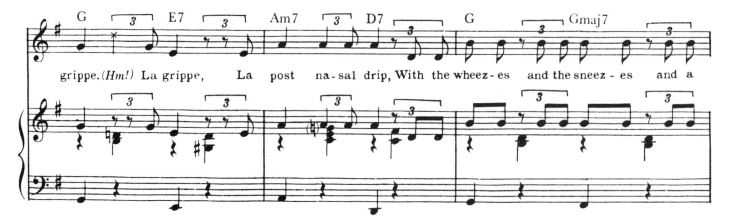

grippe. *(Hm!)* La grippe, La post na-sal drip, With the wheez-es and the sneez-es and a

si-nus that's real-ly a pip! From a lack of com-mun-i-ty prop-er-ty___ and a

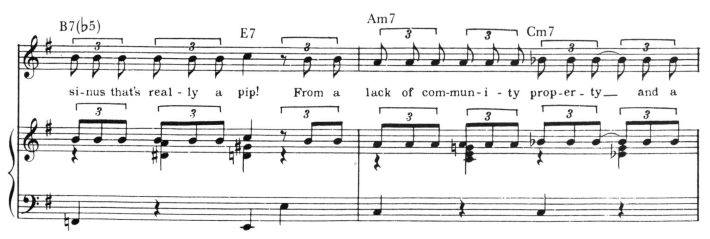

feel-ing she's get-ting too old, A per-son___ can de-vel-op a

bad, bad cold.

AIN'T MISBEHAVIN'
from AIN'T MISBEHAVIN'

Words by ANDY RAZAF
Music by THOMAS "FATS" WALLER
and HARRY BROOKS

10

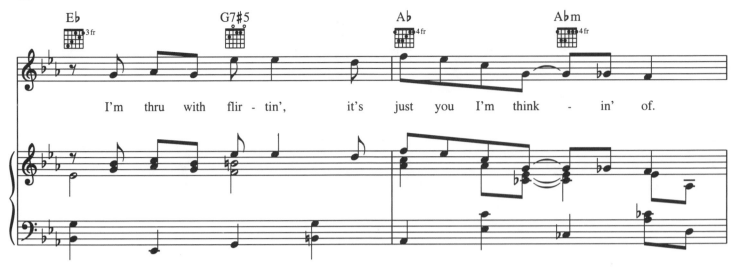

I'm thru with flir - tin', it's just you I'm think - in' of.

Ain't mis - be - hav - in, I'm sav - in' my love for you. _____

_____ Like Jack Hor - ner in the cor - ner,

don't go no - where, what do I care, Your kiss - es

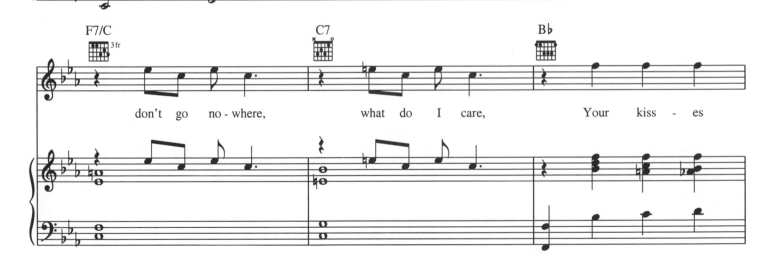

13

ALL FOR THE BEST
from the Musical GODSPELL

Words and Music by
STEPHEN SCHWARTZ

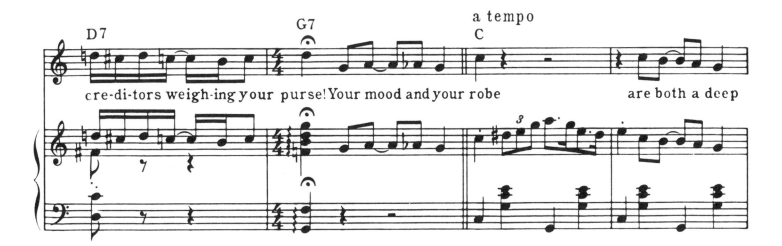

cre-di-tors weigh-ing your purse! Your mood and your robe are both a deep

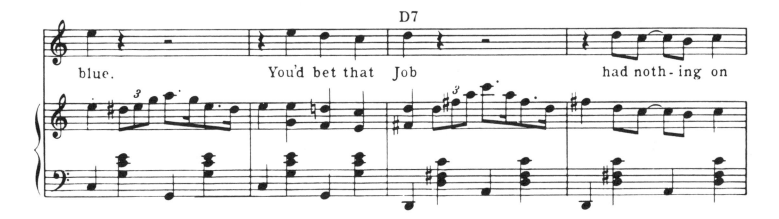

blue. You'd bet that Job had noth-ing on

you. Don't for-get that when you go to

heav-en you'll be blessed, Yes, it's all for the

Very bright 2

best.   When you feel

Some men are

sad   or - un - der a   curse

born to live at ease, do-ing what they please, rich-er than the bees are in hon -

Your life is   bad,   Your pros-pects are

- ey,   Nev-er grow-ing old, nev-er feel-ing cold, pull-ing pots of

18

AND ALL THAT JAZZ
from CHICAGO

Words by FRED EBB
Music by JOHN KANDER

BEAUTY AND THE BEAST

from Walt Disney's BEAUTY AND THE BEAST: THE BROADWAY MUSICAL

Lyrics by HOWARD ASHMAN
Music by ALAN MENKEN

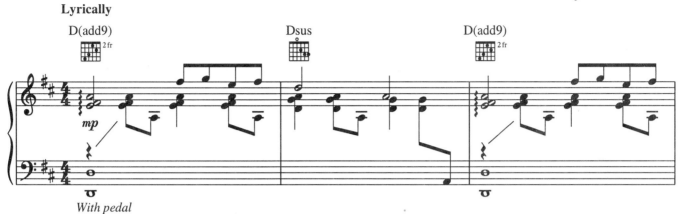

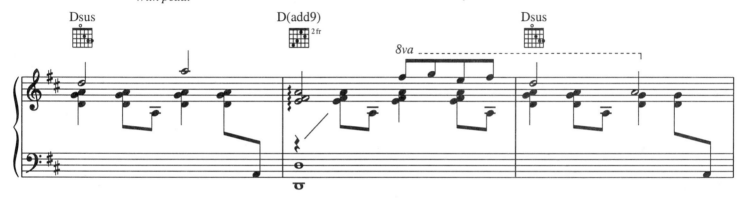

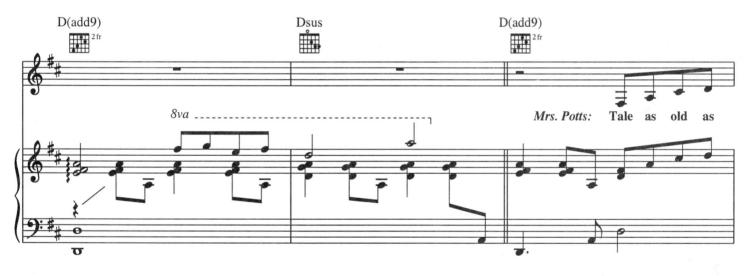

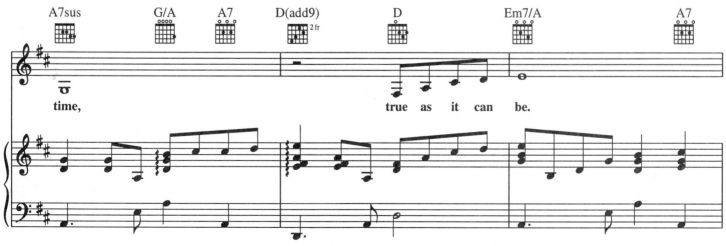

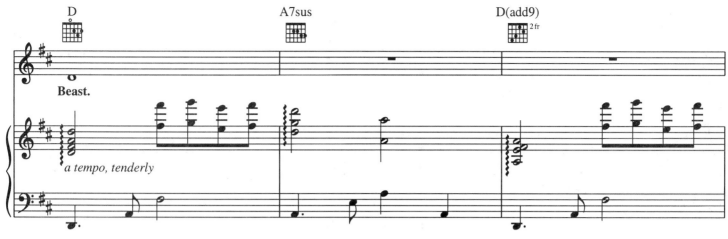

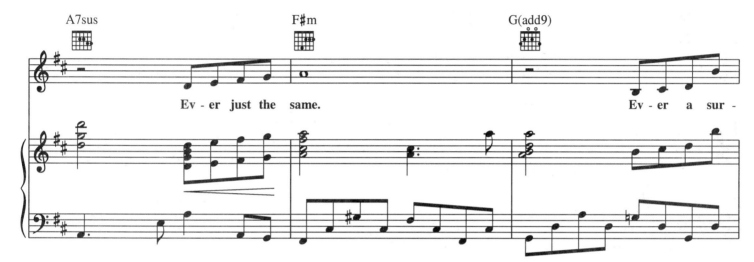

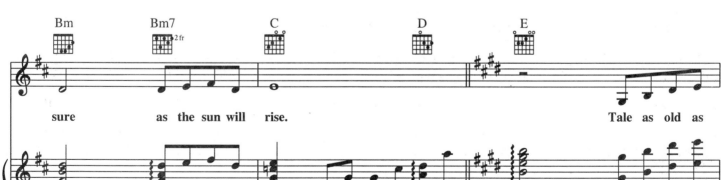

As If We Never Said Goodbye

from SUNSET BOULEVARD

Music by ANDREW LLOYD WEBBER
Lyrics by DON BLACK and CHRISTOPHER HAMPTON,
with contributions by AMY POWERS

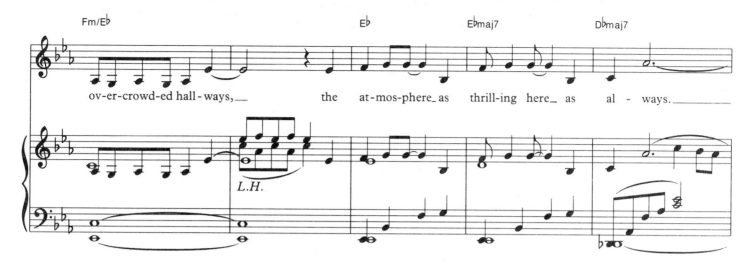

ov-er-crowd-ed hall-ways,__ the at-mos-phere_ as thrill-ing here_ as al - ways.__

__ Feel the ear-ly morn-ing mad - ness,__ feel the ma-gic in the mak - ing.__ Why,

ev-ery-thing's as if we ne - ver said good - bye._____ I've

spent so ma-ny morn-ings,__ just try-ing to re-sist you.__ I'm trem-bling now,_ you

32

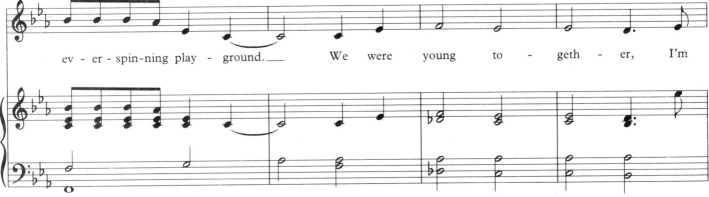

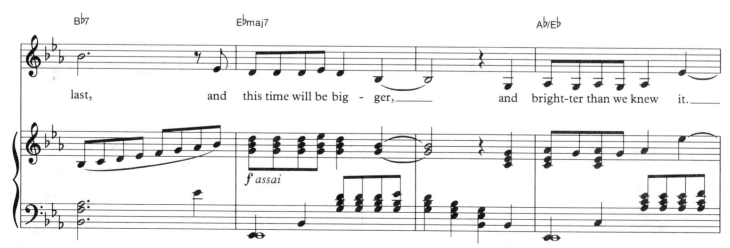

So watch me fly,__ we all know I__ can do it._____ Could I

stop my hand from shak - ing?_____ Has there ev - er been a mo - ment____ with so

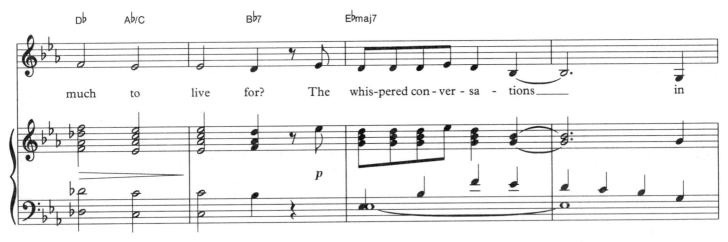

much to live for? The whis-pered con - ver - sa - tions____ in

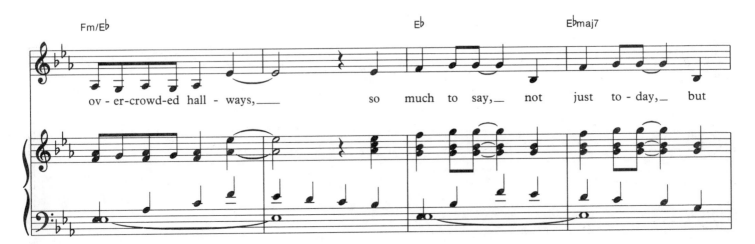

ov - er-crowd-ed hall - ways,____ so much to say,__ not just to - day,__ but

al - ways._____ We'll have ear-ly morn-ing mad - ness,_____ we'll have

ma-gic in the mak - ing,_____ yes, ev-ery-thing's as if we ne - ver said good -

bye,_____ yes, ev-ery-thing's as if we ne - ver said good - bye._____

_ We taught the world new ways to dream.

BOSOM BUDDIES
from MAME

Music and Lyric by
JERRY HERMAN

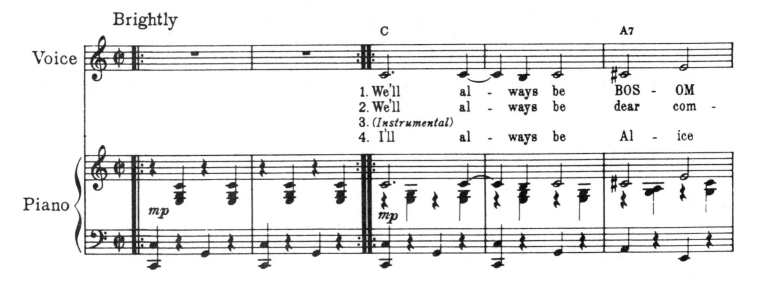

1. We'll al - ways be BOS - OM
2. We'll al - ways be dear com -
3. (Instrumental)
4. I'll al - ways be Al - ice

BUD - DIES, friends, sis - ters and pals;
pan - ions, my cro - ny, my mate;
Tok - las, if you'll be Ger - trude Stein.

We'll al - ways be BOS - OM BUD - DIES, If life should re - ject
We'll al - ways be har - mo - niz - ing, Or - phan An - nie and Sand -
And tho' I'll ad - mit I've dished you, I've gos - siped and gloat -

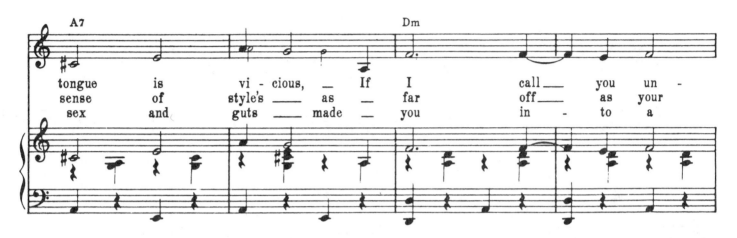

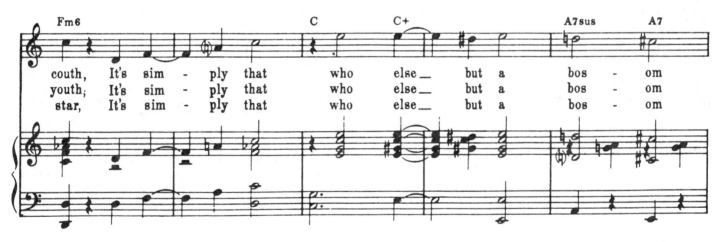

⊕ Coda

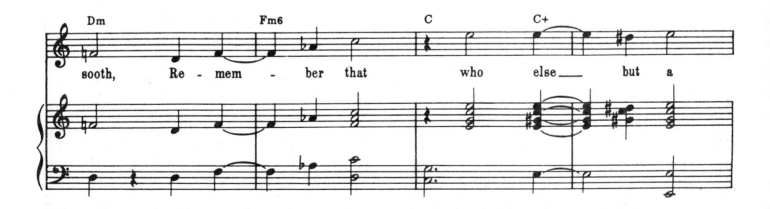

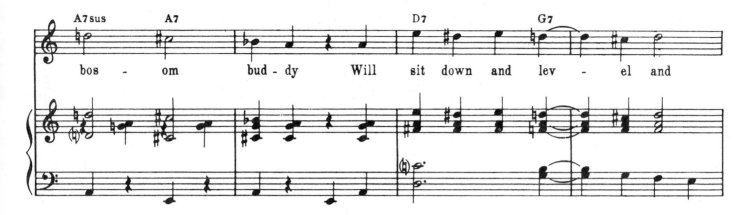

bos - om bud - dy Will sit down and lev - el and

give you the dev - il, Will sit down and

tell you the truth!

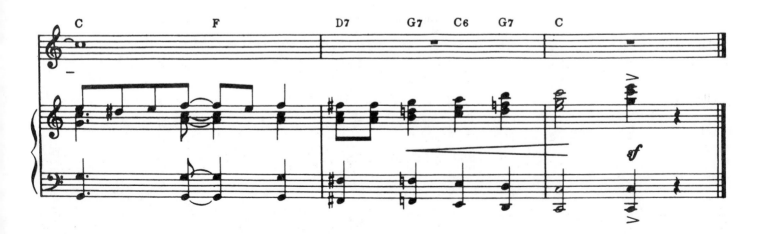

CABARET
from the Musical CABARET

Words by FRED EBB
Music by JOHN KANDER

What good is sit - ting a - lone in your room? _
Put down the knit - ting, the book and the broom, _

Come hear the mu - sic play; _____
Time for a hol - i - day; _____

Life is a cab - a - ret, old chum, _ Come to the

42

BRING HIM HOME

from LES MISÉRABLES

Music by CLAUDE-MICHEL SCHÖNBERG
Lyrics by HERBERT KRETZMER and ALAIN BOUBLIL

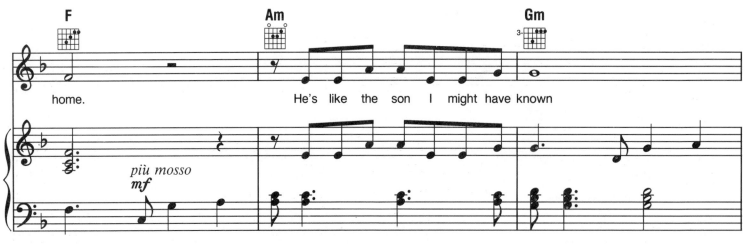

home. He's like the son I might have known

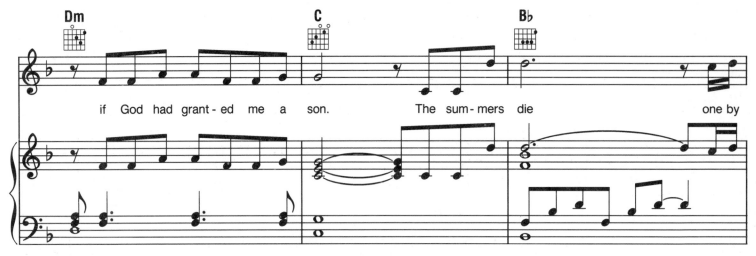

if God had grant-ed me a son. The sum-mers die one by

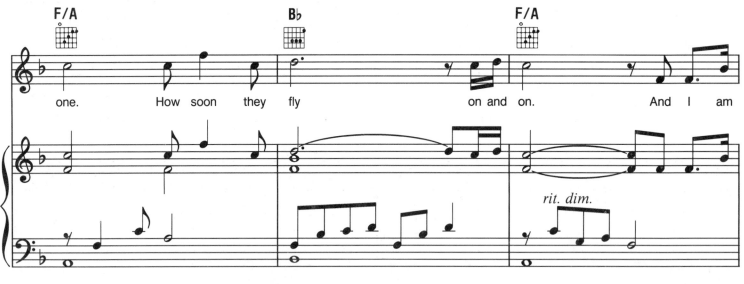

one. How soon they fly on and on. And I am

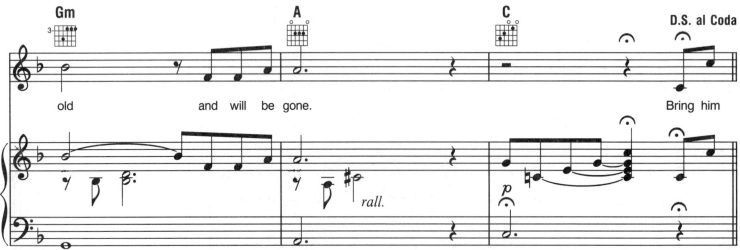

old and will be gone. Bring him

BROTHERHOOD OF MAN
from HOW TO SUCCEED IN BUSINESS WITHOUT REALLY TRYING

By FRANK LOESSER

Handclapping Spiritual Feel

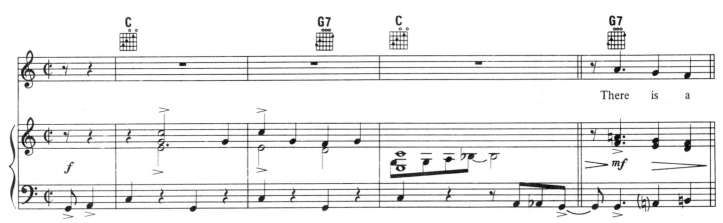

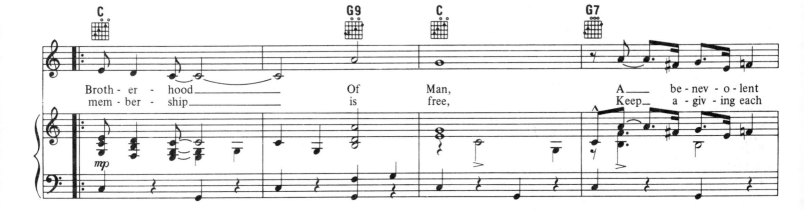

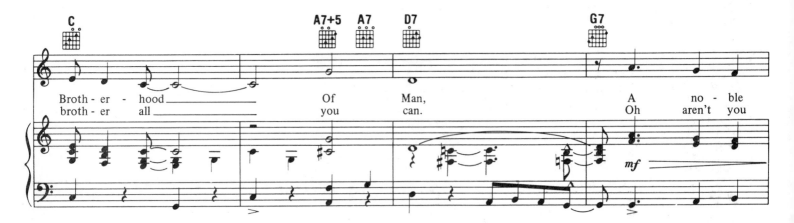

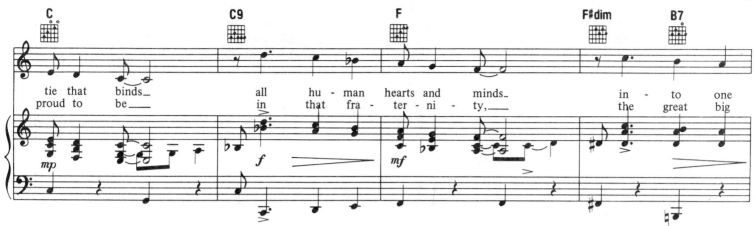

tie that binds_ all hu-man hearts and minds_ in-to one
proud to be_ in that fra-ter-ni-ty, the great big

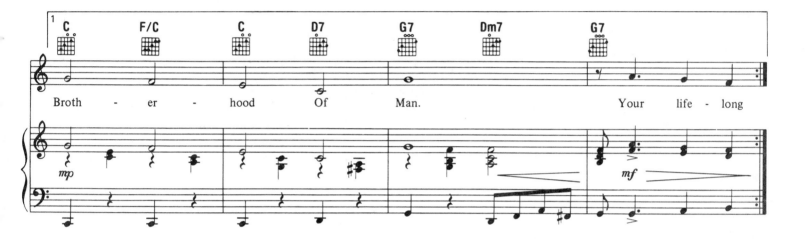

Broth - er - hood Of Man. Your life-long

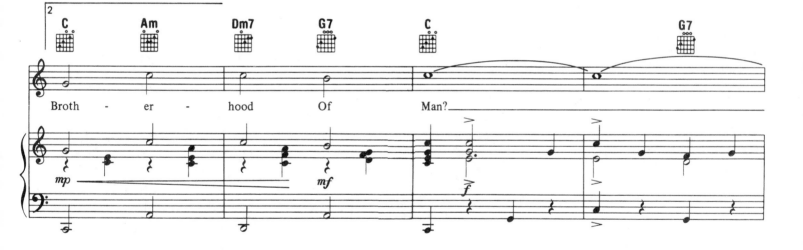

Broth - er - hood Of Man?

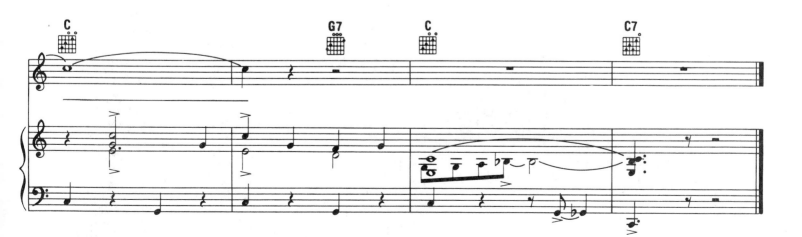

CLOSE EVERY DOOR

from JOSEPH AND THE AMAZING TECHNICOLOR® DREAMCOAT

Music by ANDREW LLOYD WEBBER
Lyrics by TIM RICE

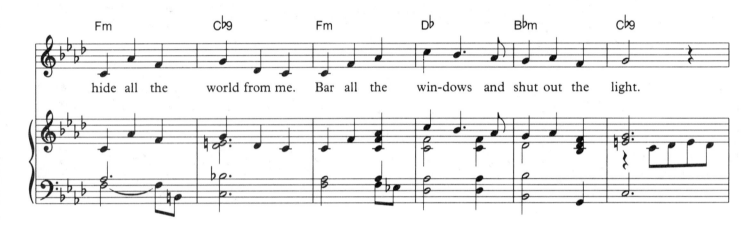

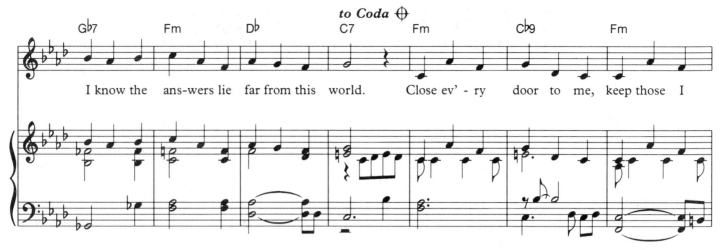

I know the ans-wers lie far from this world. Close ev' - ry door to me, keep those I

love from me. Child - ren of Is - rael are nev-er a - lone. For I know I shall

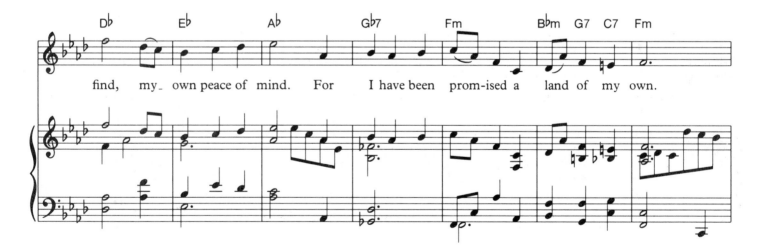

find, my_ own peace of mind. For I have been prom-ised a land of my own.

CHORUS

Close ev' - ry door to me, hide all the world from me. Bar all the

52

win-dows and shut out the light. la la la la la la la la la la la la

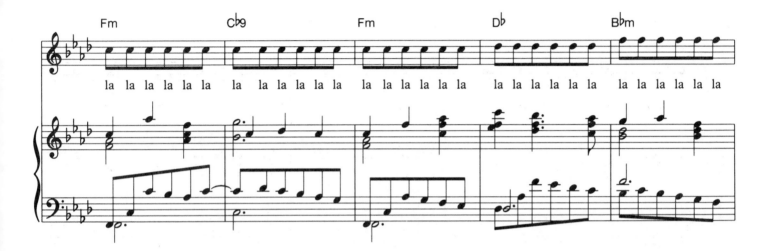

la la la la la la la la la la la la la la la la la la la la la la la la la la la la la la

la.

JOSEPH

Just give me a num-ber in-stead of a

name. For - get all a - bout me and let me de - cay.

Close ev' - ry door to me, hide those I love from me. Child - ren of

Is - rael are nev - er a - lone. For we know we shall find our __

own peace of mind. For we have been pro - mised a land __ of our own.

DO-RE-MI
from THE SOUND OF MUSIC

Lyrics by OSCAR HAMMERSTEIN II
Music by RICHARD RODGERS

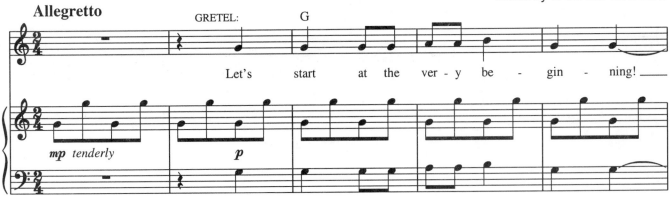

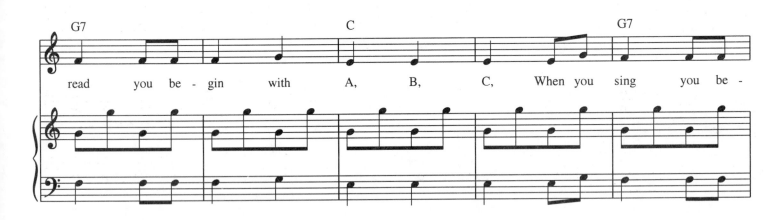

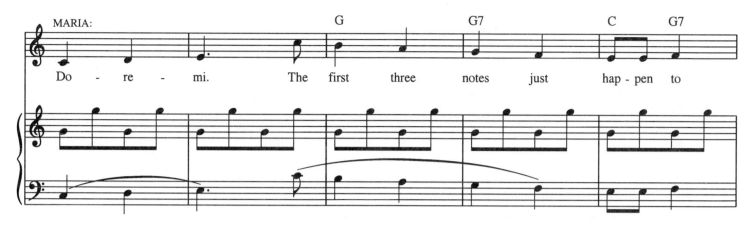

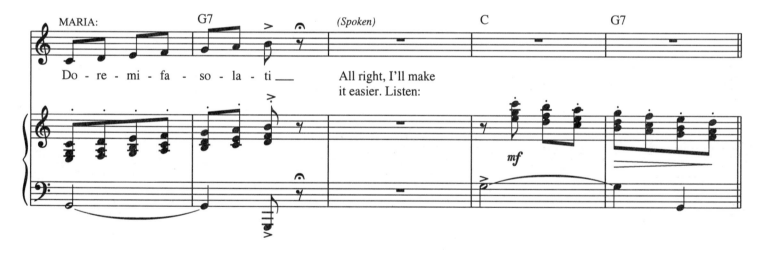

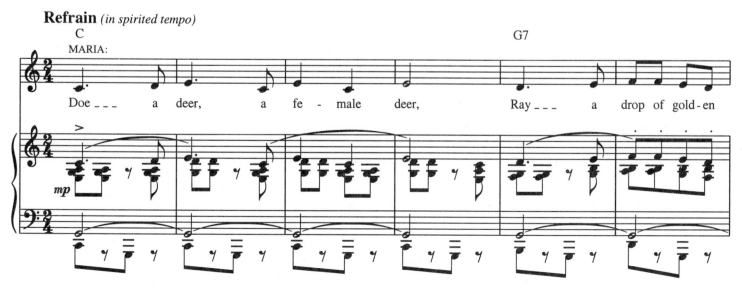

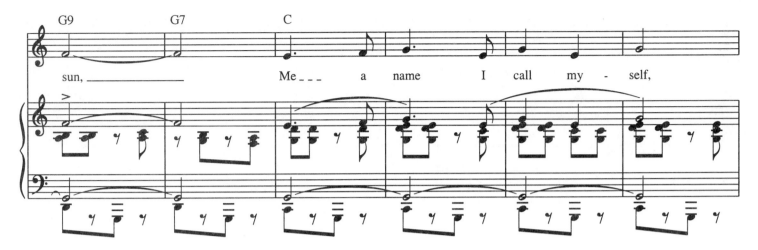

sun, _____ Me _ _ _ a name I call my - self,

Far _ _ _ a long, long way to run. _____ Sew _ _ _ a nee - dle pull - ing

thread, _____ La _ _ _ a note to fol - low sew, _____

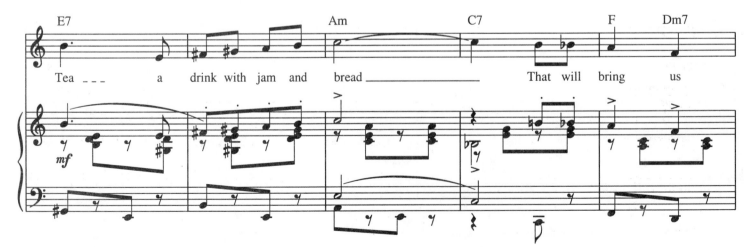

Tea _ _ _ a drink with jam and bread _____ That will bring us

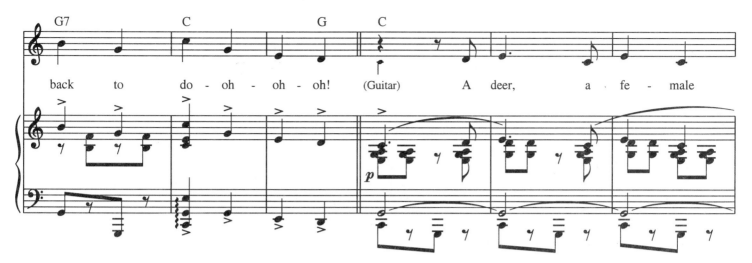

back to do - oh - oh - oh! (Guitar) A deer, a fe - male

CHILDREN:
(spoken) G7   MARIA: G9   G7   CHILDREN:

deer, Do! (Guitar) A drop of gold - en sun, _____ Re!

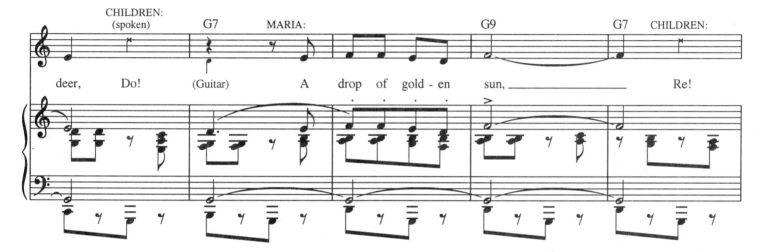

C   MARIA: CHILDREN: G9   MARIA:

(Guitar) A name I call my - self, Mi! (Guitar) A

G9   C   C7
                     CHILDREN: MARIA:
                                (sung) CHILDREN:

long, long way to run, _____ Fa! So! A nee - dle pull - ing

poco a poco cresc.

58

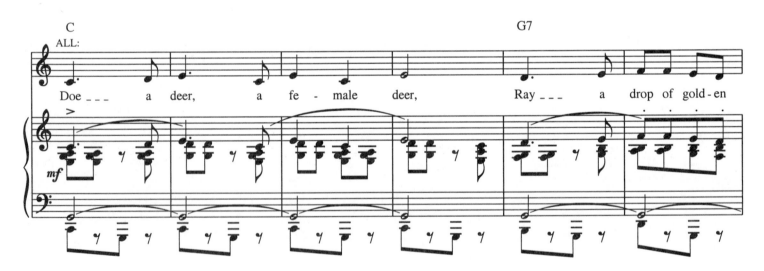

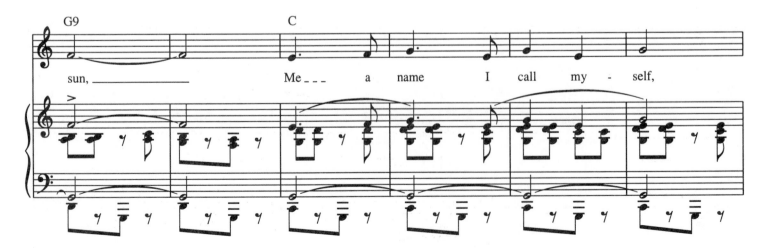

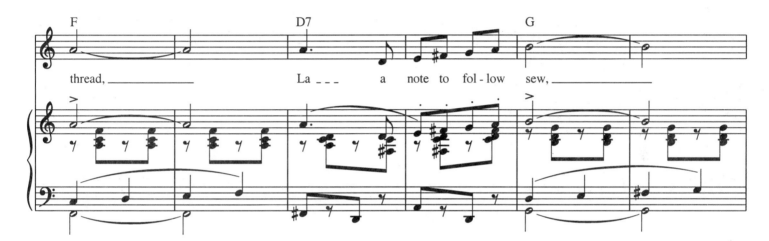

COMEDY TONIGHT
from A FUNNY THING HAPPENED ON THE WAY TO THE FORUM

Words and Music by
STEPHEN SONDHEIM

Brightly

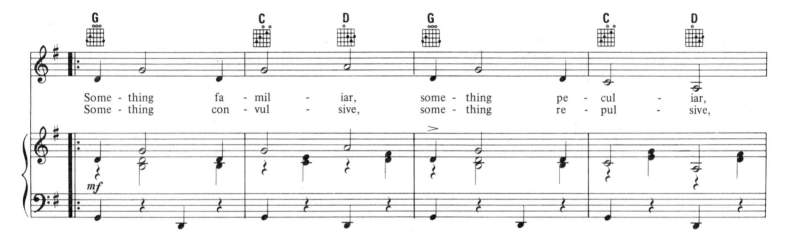

Some - thing fa - mil - iar, some - thing pe - cul - iar,
Some - thing con - vul - sive, some - thing re - pul - sive,

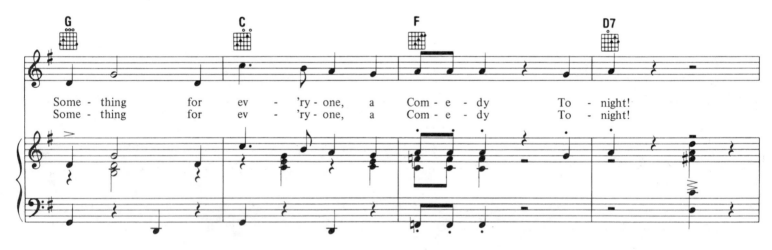

Some - thing for ev - 'ry - one, a Com - e - dy To - night!
Some - thing for ev - 'ry - one, a Com - e - dy To - night!

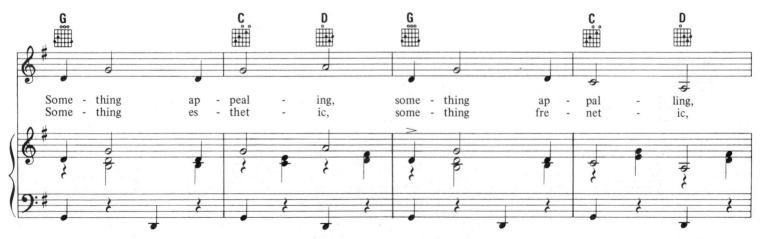

Some - thing ap - peal - ing, some - thing ap - pal - ling,
Some - thing es - thet - ic, some - thing fre - net - ic,

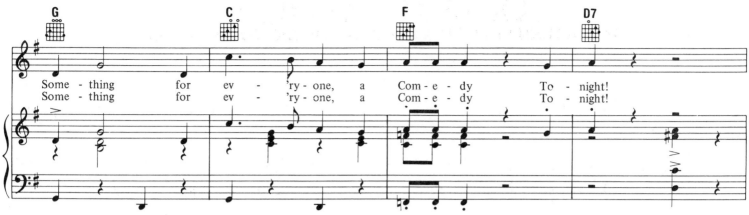

Some - thing for ev - 'ry - one, a Com - e - dy To - night!
Some - thing for ev - 'ry - one, a Com - e - dy To - night!

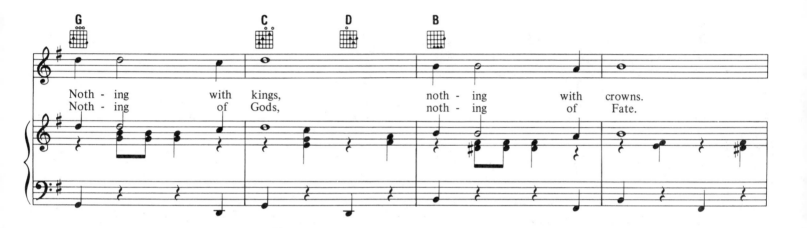

Noth - ing with kings, noth - ing with crowns.
Noth - ing of Gods, noth - ing of Fate.

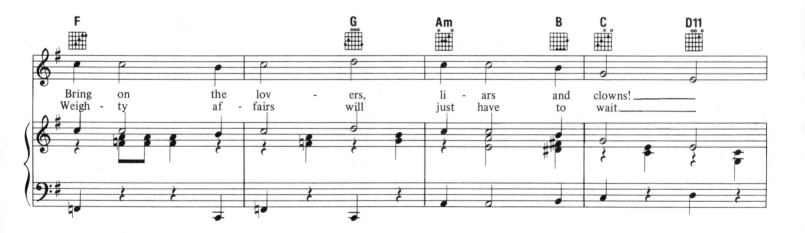

Bring on the lov - ers, li - ars and clowns! _____
Weight - y af - fairs will just have to wait. _____

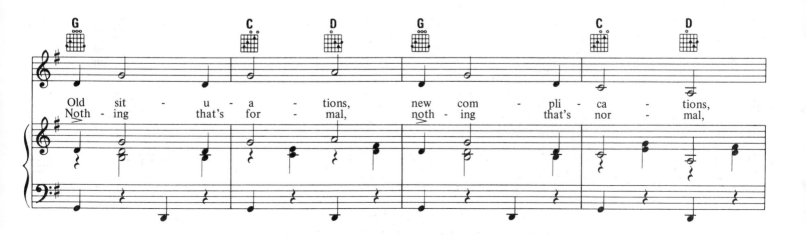

Old sit - u - a - tions, new com - pli - ca - tions,
Noth - ing that's for - mal, noth - ing that's nor - mal,

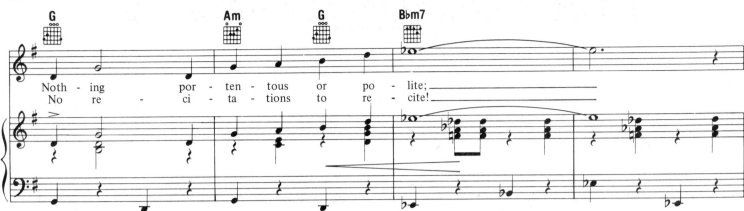

Nothing por-ten-tous or po-lite;_____
No re-ci-ta-tions to re-cite!_____

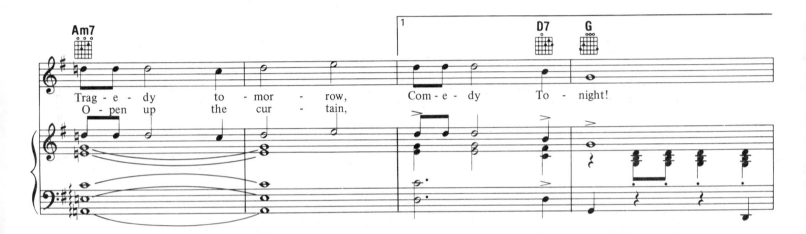

Trag-e-dy to-mor-row,   Com-e-dy To-night!
O-pen up the cur-tain,

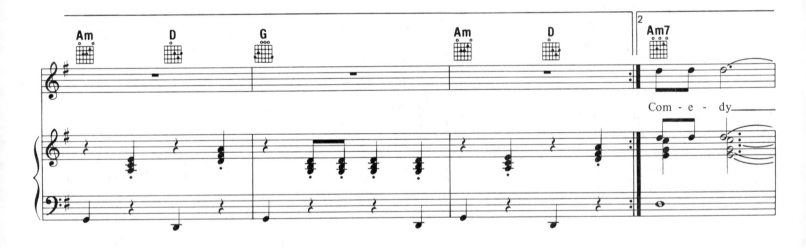

Com-e-dy____

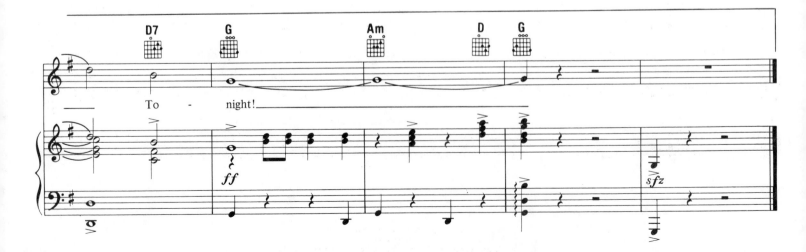

To - night!____

DON'T RAIN ON MY PARADE

from FUNNY GIRL

Words by BOB MERRILL
Music by JULE STYNE

Don't tell me not to fly, I've sim-ply got to. If some-one takes a spill, it's me and not you.

Don't bring a-round a cloud To rain on my pa-rade.

Don't tell me not to live, just sit and put-ter. Life's can-dy and the sun's a ball of but-ter.

EASTER PARADE

from AS THOUSANDS CHEER

Words and Music by
IRVING BERLIN

GET ME TO THE CHURCH ON TIME

from MY FAIR LADY

Words by ALAN JAY LERNER
Music by FREDERICK LOEWE

Brightly

I'm get-ting mar-ried in the morn-ing _____ Ding! dong! the

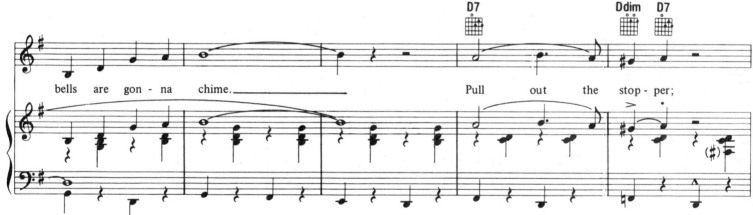

bells are gon-na chime. _____ Pull out the stop-per;

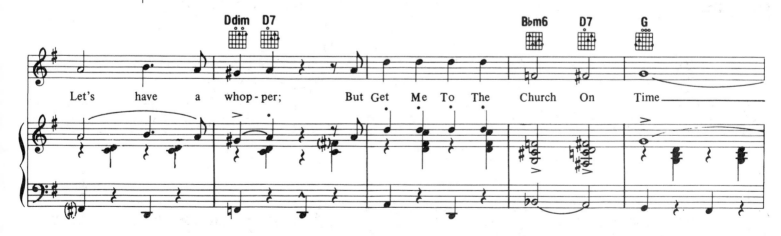

Let's have a whop-per; But Get Me To The Church On Time _____

72

GIVE MY REGARDS TO BROADWAY

from LITTLE JOHNNY JONES

Words and Music by
GEORGE M. COHAN

75

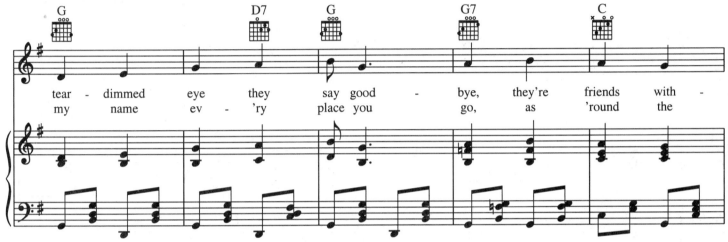

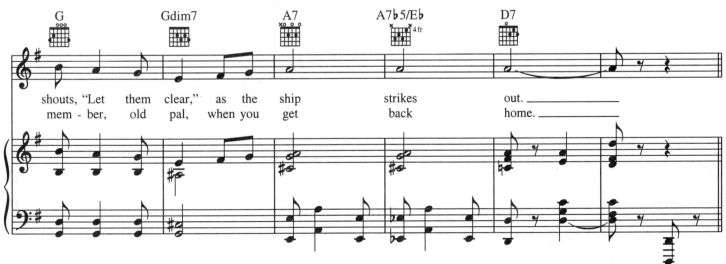

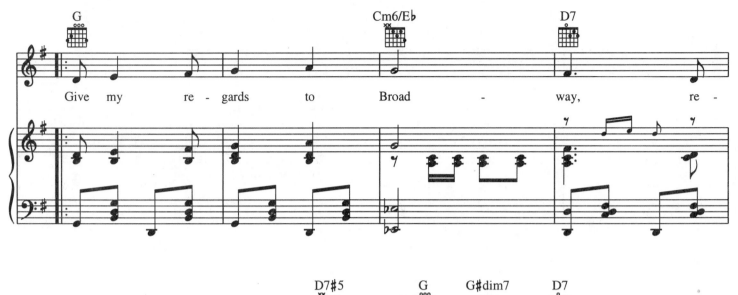

Give my re- gards to Broad - way, re-

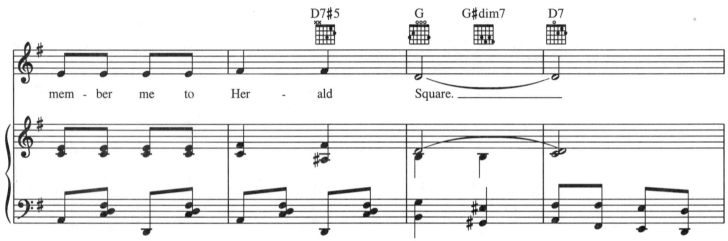

mem - ber me to Her - ald Square. _____

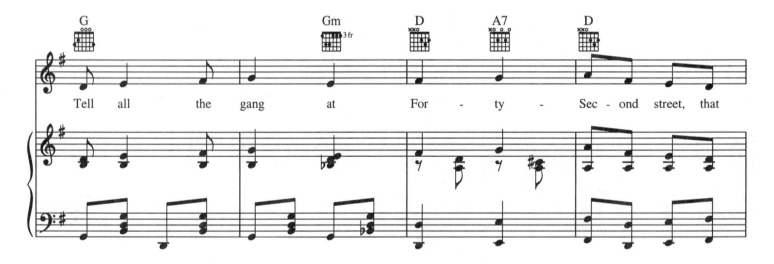

Tell all the gang at For - ty - Sec- ond street, that

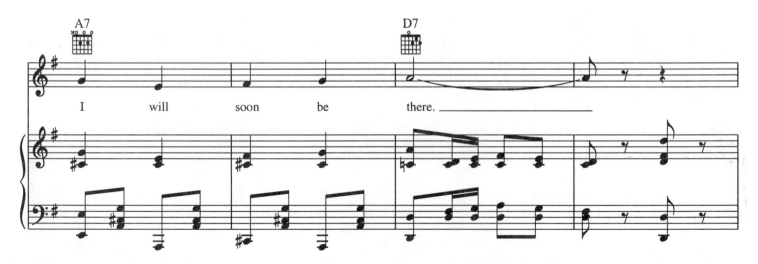

I will soon be there. _____

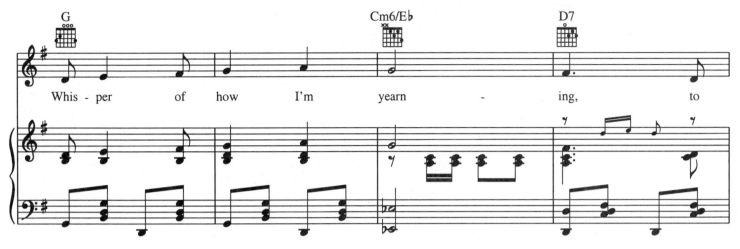

Whis - per of how I'm yearn - ing, to

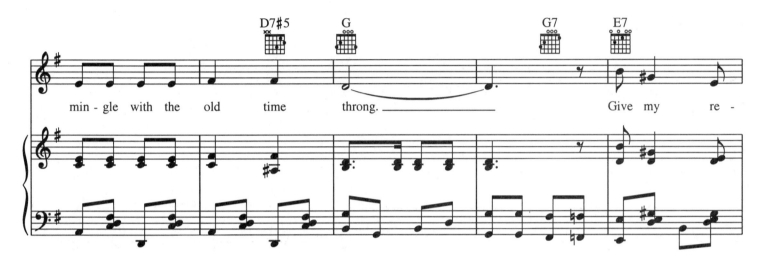

min - gle with the old time throng. _____ Give my re -

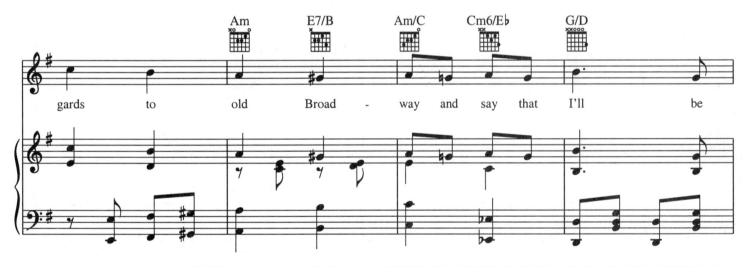

gards to old Broad - way and say that I'll be

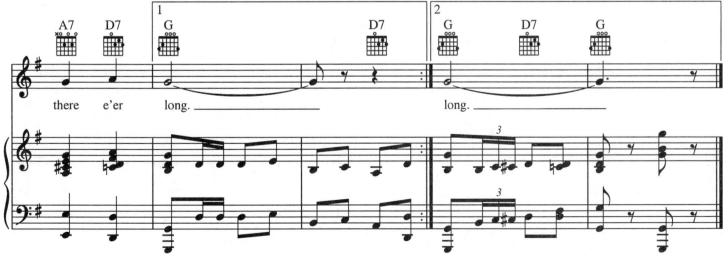

there e'er long. _____ long. _____

GLAD TO BE UNHAPPY
from ON YOUR TOES

Words by LORENZ HART
Music by RICHARD RODGERS

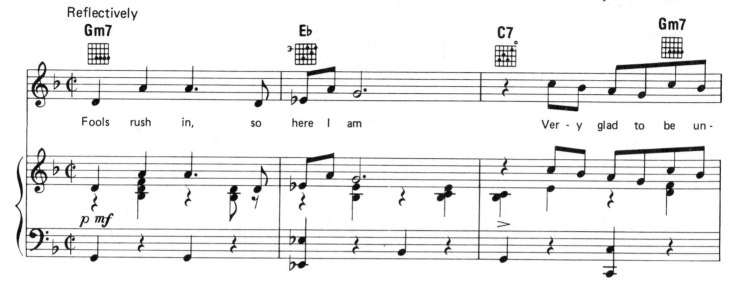

Fools rush in, so here I am Ver - y glad to be un-

hap - py; ____ I can't win, but here I am, More than glad to be un-

hap - py. ____ Un - re - qui - ted love's a bore. And I've got it pret - ty

GODSPEED TITANIC
(Sail On)
from TITANIC

Music and Lyrics by
MAURY YESTON

81

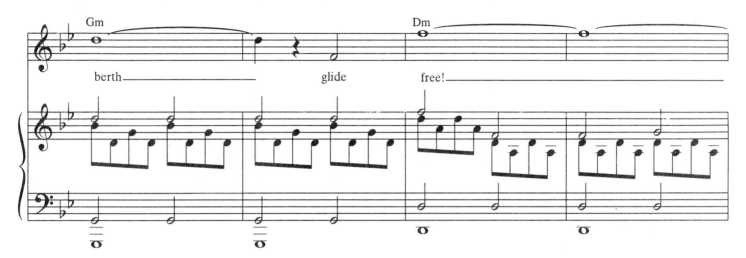

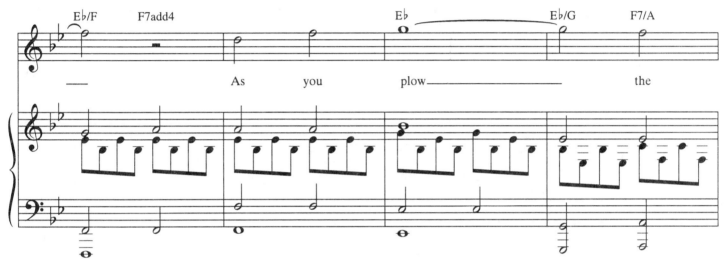

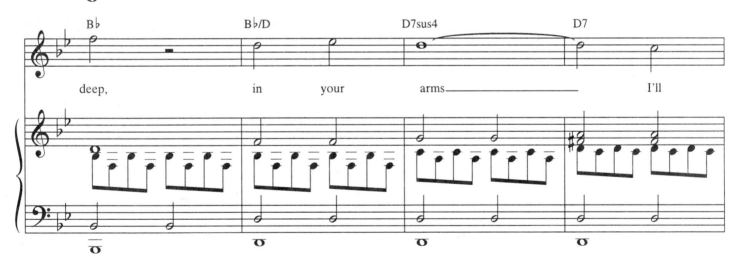

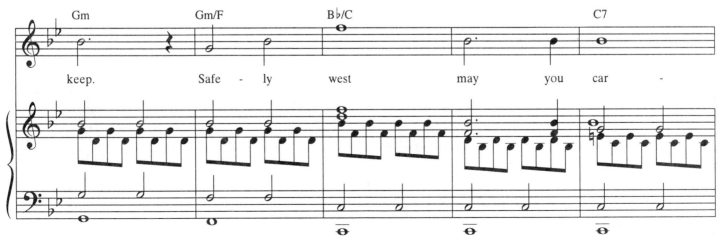

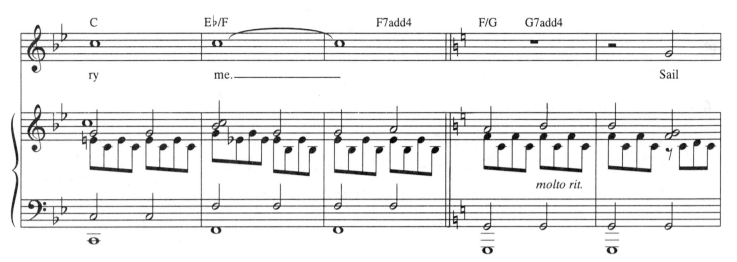

C   Eb/F   F7add4   F/G   G7add4

ry   me._____   Sail

molto rit.

C   G/B   Am   Em

on,_____   sail   on,_____   great   ship_____

F   G7sus4   C   G/B

____   *Ti - tan - ic.*____   Cross____   the

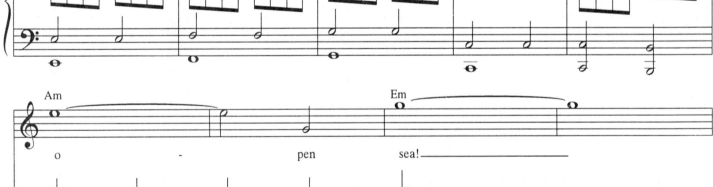

Am   Em

o -   pen   sea!_____

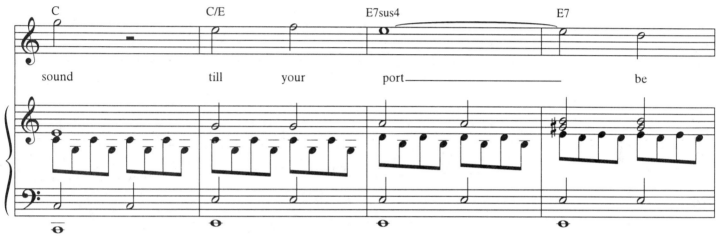

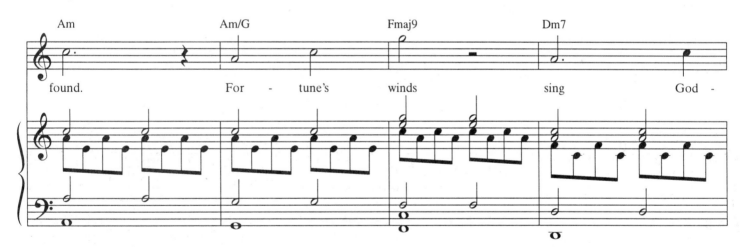

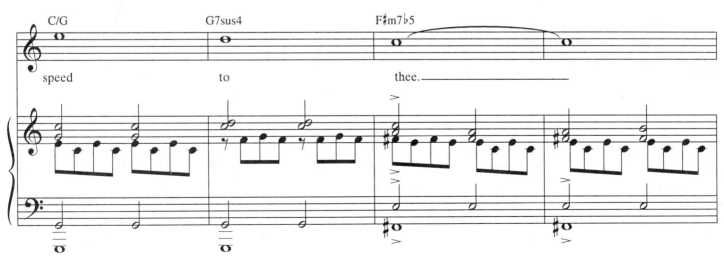

I ENJOY BEING A GIRL
from FLOWER DRUM SONG

Lyrics by OSCAR HAMMERSTEIN II
Music by RICHARD RODGERS

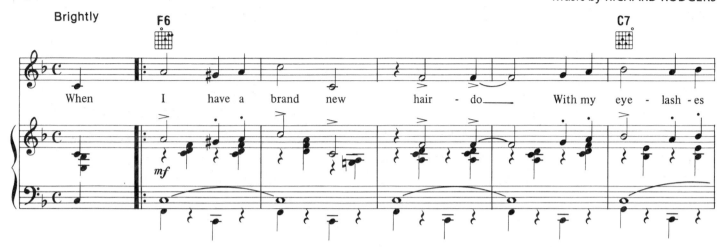

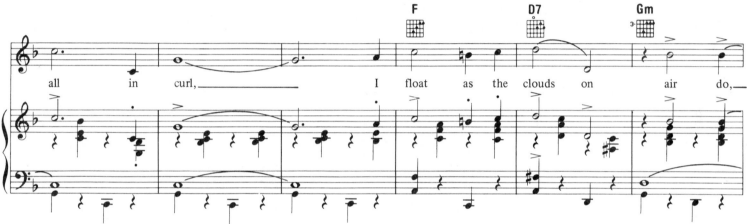

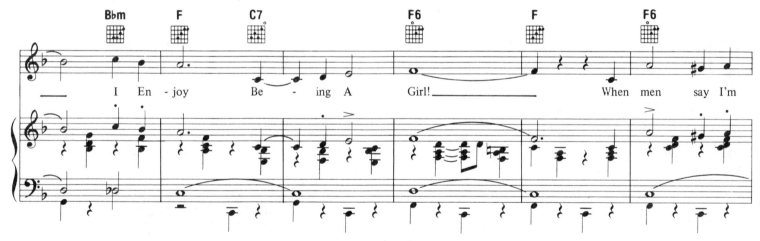

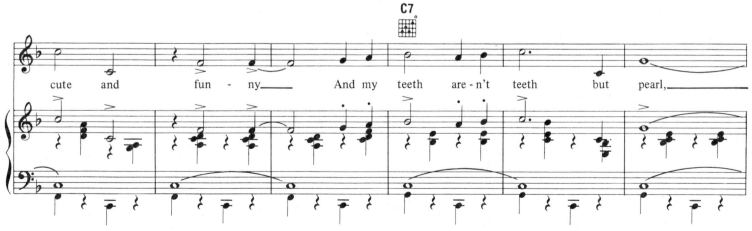

GOODNIGHT, MY SOMEONE

from Meredith Willson's THE MUSIC MAN

By MEREDITH WILLSON

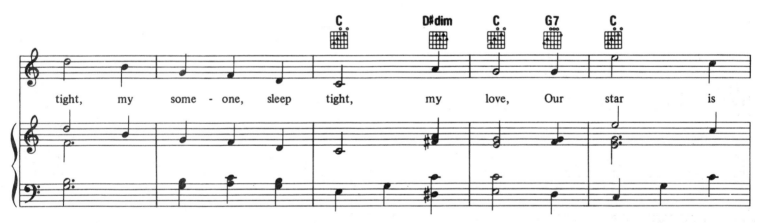

night. _____ Sweet dreams be yours dear if dreams there

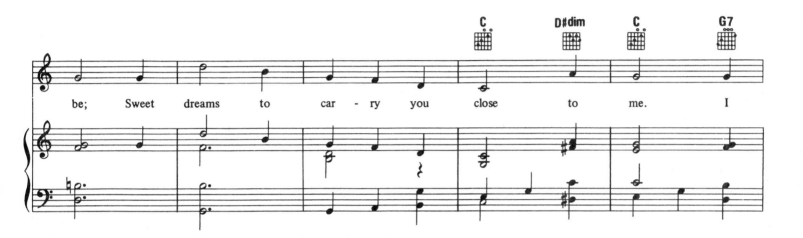

be; Sweet dreams to car - ry you close to me. I

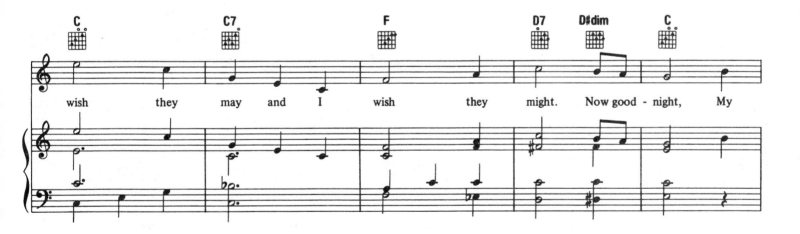

wish they may and I wish they might. Now good - night, My

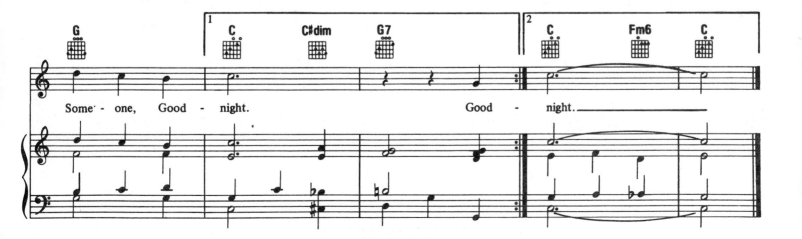

Some - one, Good - night. Good - night. _____

HELLO, DOLLY!

from HELLO, DOLLY!

Music and Lyric by
JERRY HERMAN

I AIN'T DOWN YET

from THE UNSINKABLE MOLLY BROWN

By MEREDITH WILLSON

March tempo

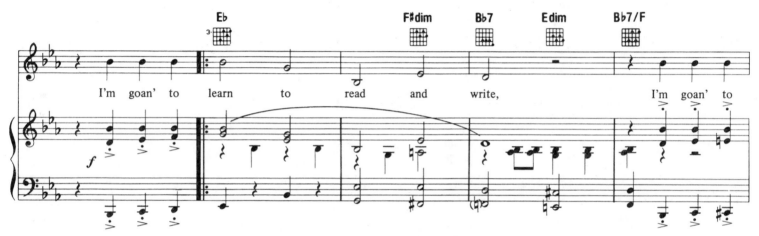

I'm goan' to learn to read and write, I'm goan' to

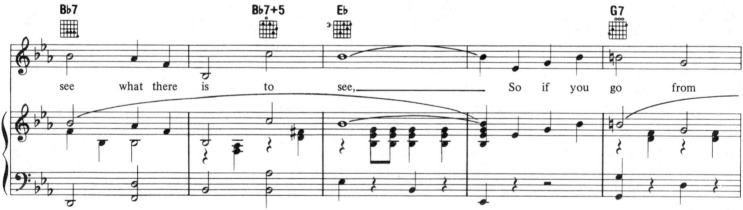

see what there is to see, So if you go from

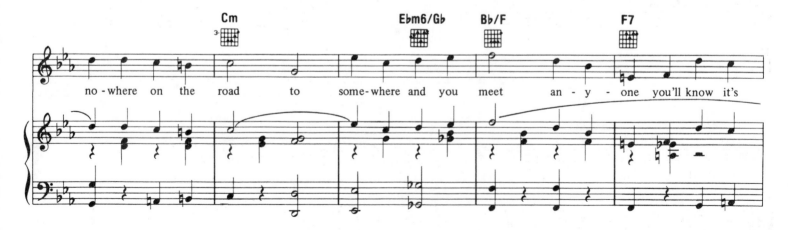

no-where on the road to some-where and you meet an-y-one you'll know it's

I HAVE DREAMED
from THE KING AND I

Lyrics by OSCAR HAMMERSTEIN II
Music by RICHARD RODGERS

I WISH I WERE IN LOVE AGAIN

from BABES IN ARMS

Words by LORENZ HART
Music by RICHARD RODGERS

I'D DO ANYTHING
from the Broadway Musical OLIVER!

Words and Music by
LIONEL BART

ev - 'ry -thing   for   one   kiss   ev - 'ry -thing;   Yes,
ev - 'ry -thing   for   one   kiss   ev - 'ry -thing;   Yes,
life   and   limb   To   keep   you   in   the   swim;   Yes,

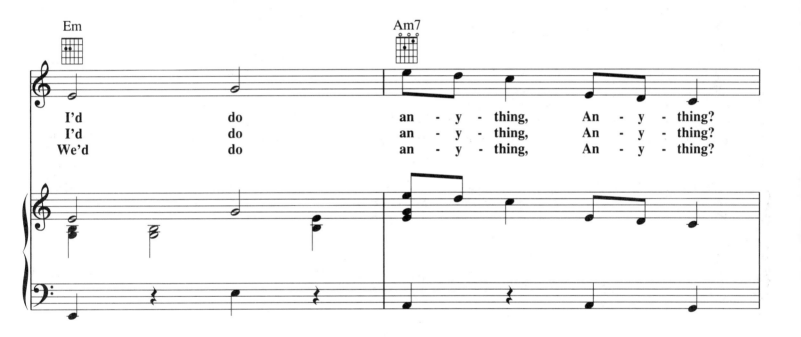

I'd   do   an - y - thing,   An - y - thing?
I'd   do   an - y - thing,   An - y - thing?
We'd   do   an - y - thing,   An - y - thing?

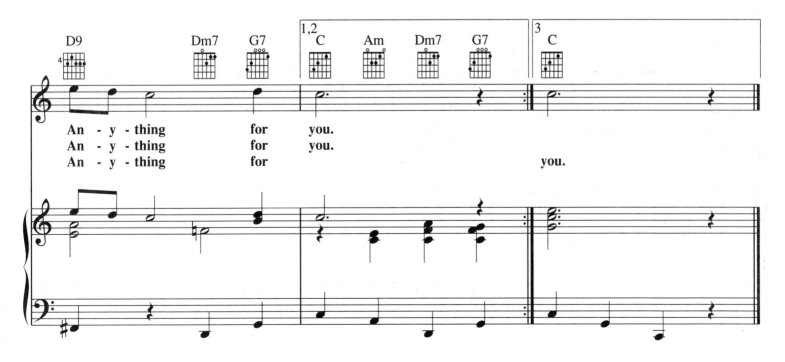

An - y -thing   for   you.
An - y -thing   for   you.
An - y -thing   for   you.

I'D GIVE MY LIFE FOR YOU

from MISS SAIGON

Music by CLAUDE-MICHEL SCHÖNBERG
Lyrics by RICHARD MALTBY JR. and ALAIN BOUBLIL
Adapted from original French Lyrics by ALAIN BOUBLIL

110

IF EVER I WOULD LEAVE YOU
from CAMELOT

Words by ALAN JAY LERNER
Music by FREDERICK LOEWE

Intro: Moderately

IF I LOVED YOU
from CAROUSEL

Lyrics by OSCAR HAMMERSTEIN II
Music by RICHARD RODGERS

Moderately fast

(Julie:) When I worked in the mill, weav-in' at the
(Billy:) Kind-a scraw-ny and pale, pick-in' at my

loom, I'd gaze ab-sent-mind-ed at the roof. _____ And
food, and love-sick like an-y oth-er guy. _____ I'd

half the time the shut-tle 'd tan-gle in the threads, and the
throw a-way my sweat-er and dress up like a dude in a

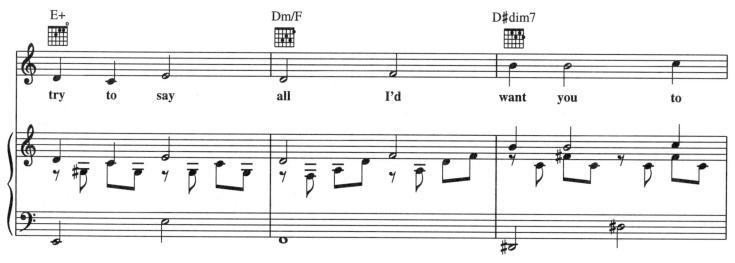

try to say   all   I'd   want you   to

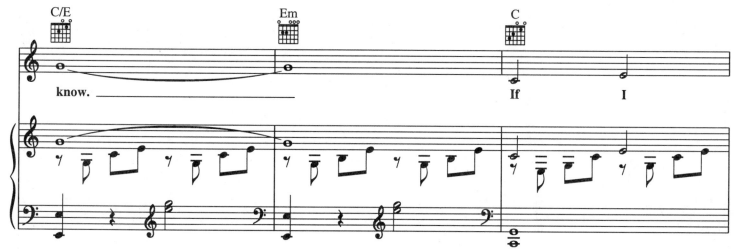

know. _____   If   I

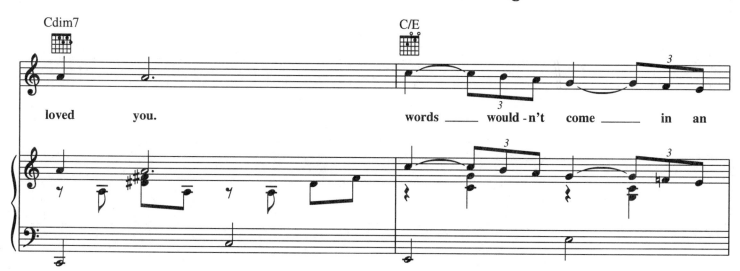

loved   you.   words ____ would-n't   come ____   in an

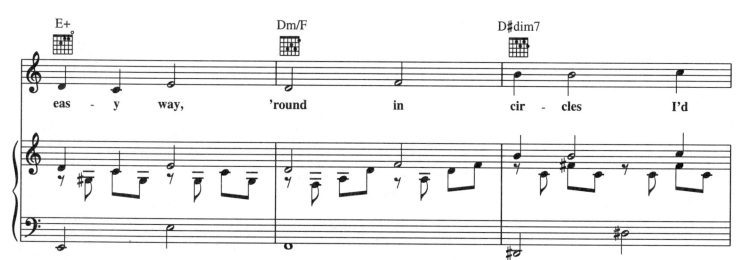

eas - y   way,   'round   in   cir - cles   I'd

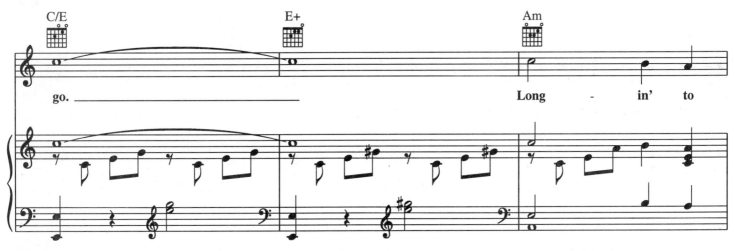

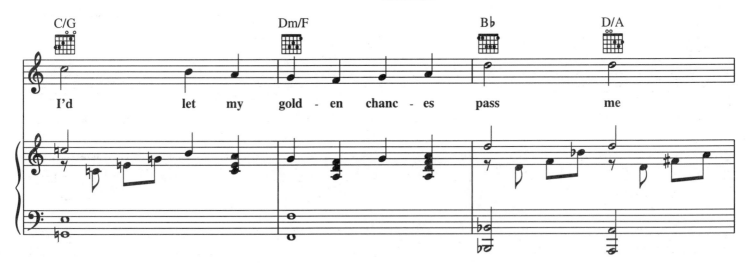

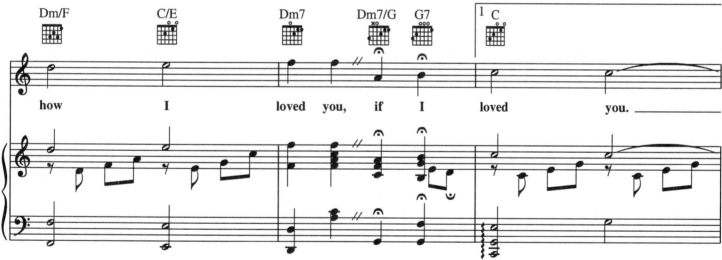

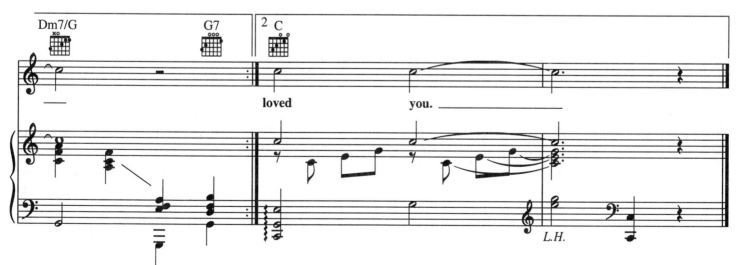

IT MIGHT AS WELL BE SPRING

from STATE FAIR

Lyrics by OSCAR HAMMERSTEIN II
Music by RICHARD RODGERS

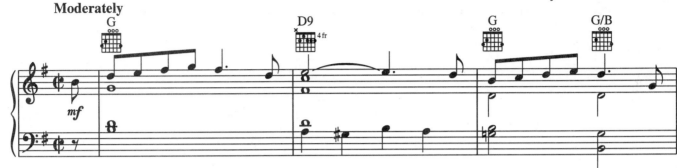

The things I used to like I don't like an-y-more. I want a lot of oth-er things I've

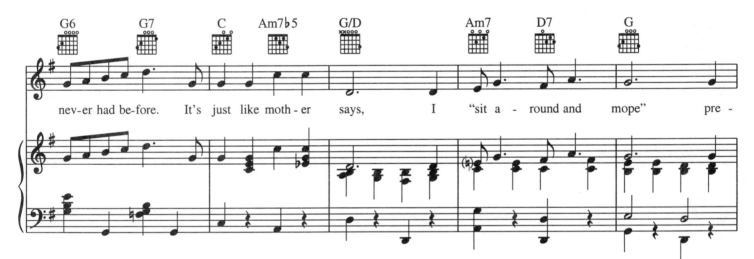

nev-er had be-fore. It's just like moth-er says, I "sit a-round and mope" pre-

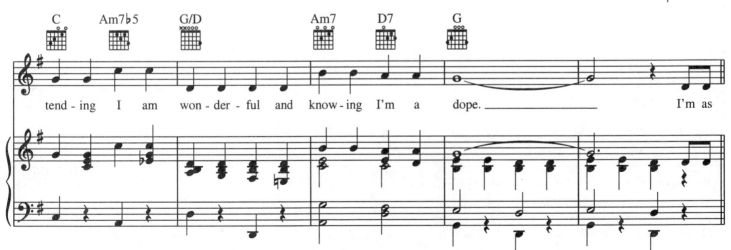

tend-ing I am won-der-ful and know-ing I'm a dope. _____ I'm as

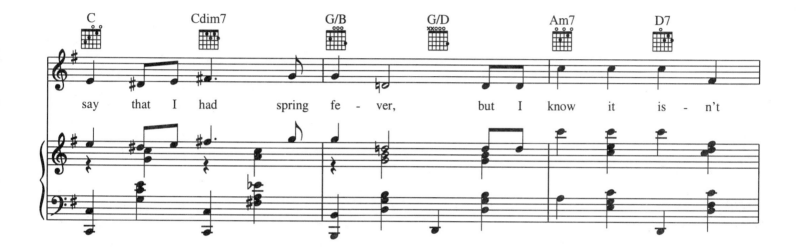

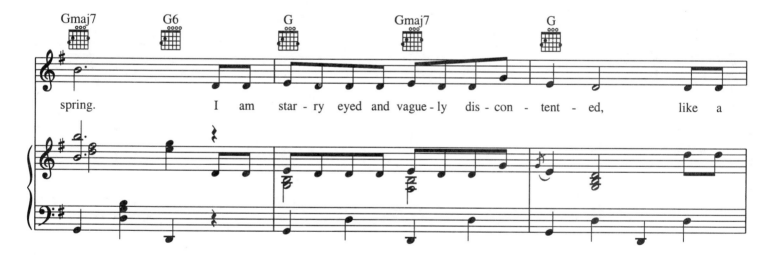

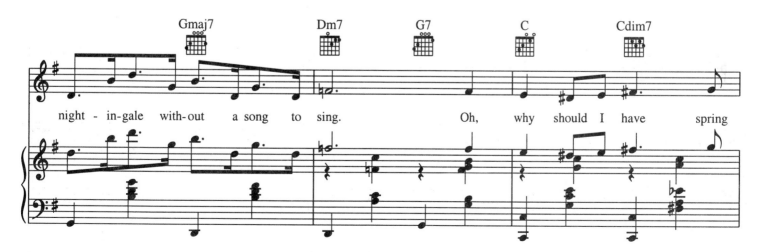

fe - ver when it is - n't e - ven spring? I keep wish-ing I were

some - where else, walk-ing down a strange new street, hear-ing words that I have

nev - er heard from a {man girl} I've yet to meet. I'm as

bus - y as a spi-der spin-ning day-dreams, I'm as gid - dy as a ba - by on a

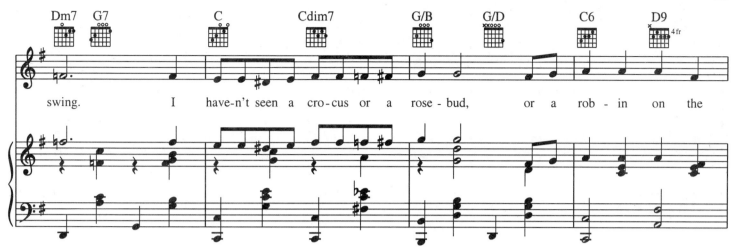

swing. I have-n't seen a cro-cus or a rose-bud, or a rob-in on the

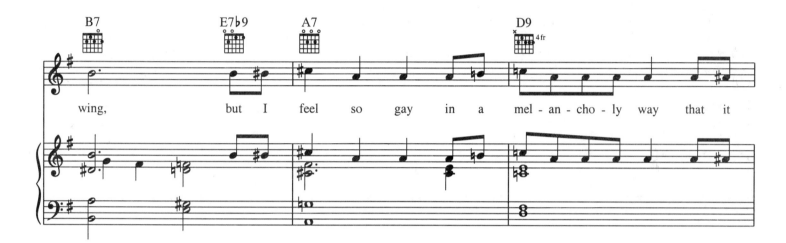

wing, but I feel so gay in a mel-an-cho-ly way that it

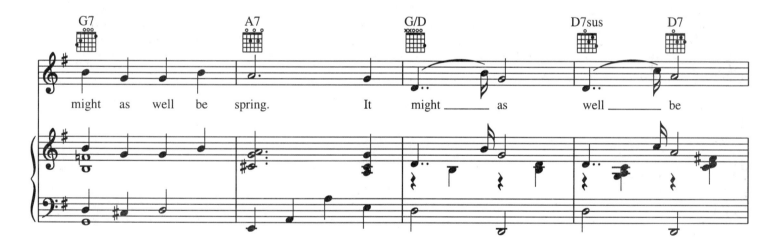

might as well be spring. It might _____ as well _____ be

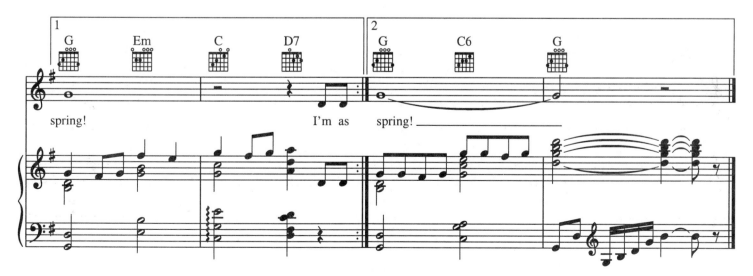

1. spring!   I'm as spring! _____

2.

THE IMPOSSIBLE DREAM
(The Quest)
from MAN OF LA MANCHA

Lyric by JOE DARION
Music by MITCH LEIGH

Tempo di Bolero

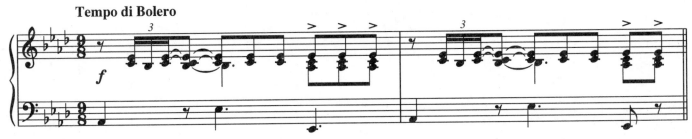

1. To dream _____ the im-pos-si-ble dream, _____ to
(2. To) right _____ the un-right-a-ble wrong, _____ to

fight _____ the un-beat-a-ble foe, _____ To
love _____ pure and chaste from a-far, _____ To

bear _____ with un-bear-a-ble sor-row, _____ to
try _____ when your arms are too wea-ry, _____ to

run _____ where the brave dare not go. _____ 2. To

reach _____ the un-reach-a-ble star! This is my

quest, _____ to fol-low that star, _____ No mat-ter how

hope-less, _____ no mat-ter how far; _____ To fight for the

right _____ with - out ques - tion or pause. _____ To be will - ing to

march in - to hell for a heav - en - ly cause! And I

know, _____ if I'll on - ly be true _____ To this glo - ri - ous

quest, _____ that my heart _____ will lie peace - ful and

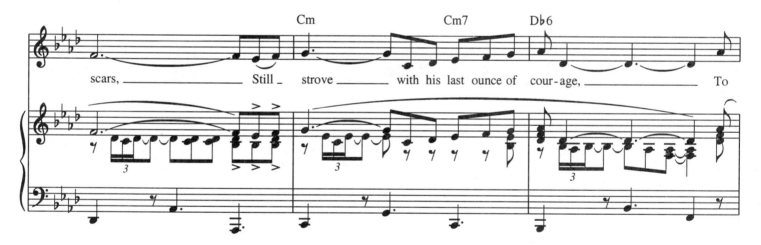

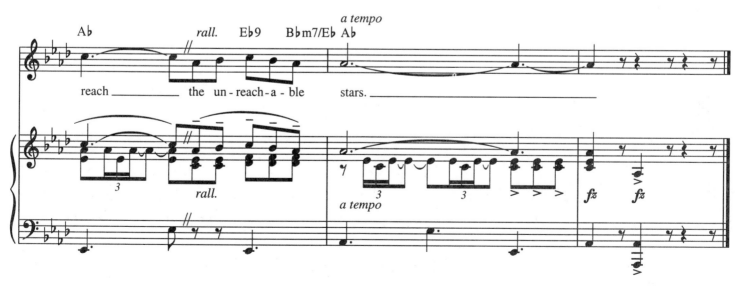

LAMBETH WALK
from ME AND MY GIRL

By NOEL GAY,
L. ARTHUR ROSE and DOUGLAS FURBER

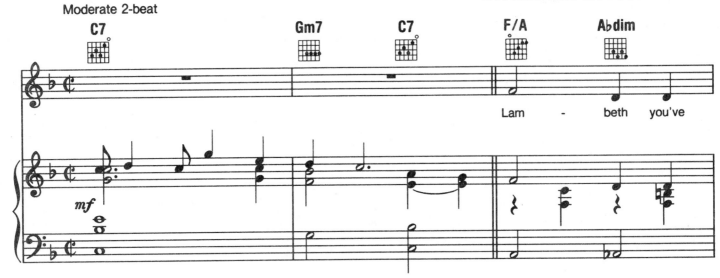

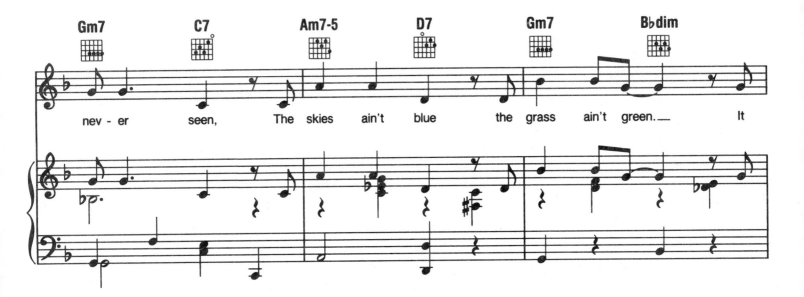

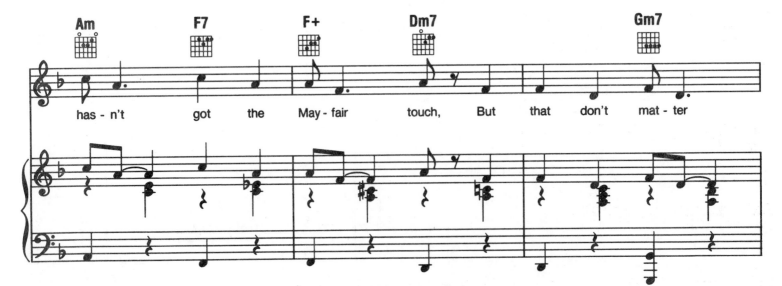

130

LAZY AFTERNOON
from THE GOLDEN APPLE

Words and Music by JOHN LATOUCHE
and JEROME MOROSS

two. _____ It's a la - zy af - ter -

noon and the farm - er leaves his reap - in', in the

mea - dow cows are sleep - in' and the speck - led trout stop leap - in' up -

stream _____ as we dream. _____

The Little Things You Do Together

from COMPANY

Music and Lyrics by
STEPHEN SONDHEIM

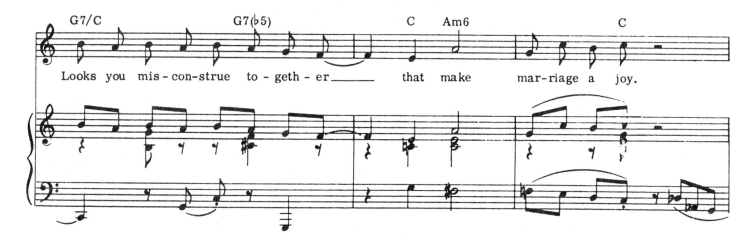

Looks you mis-con-strue to-geth-er_____ that make mar-riage a joy.

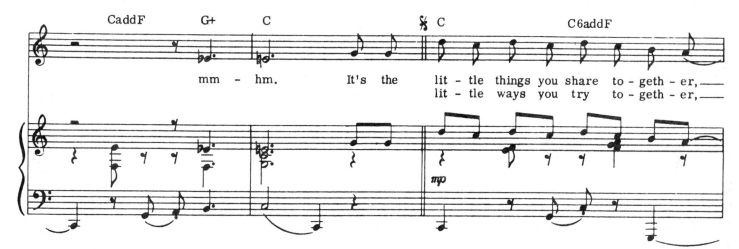

mm - hm. It's the lit - tle things you share to - geth - er,____
lit - tle ways you try to - geth - er,____

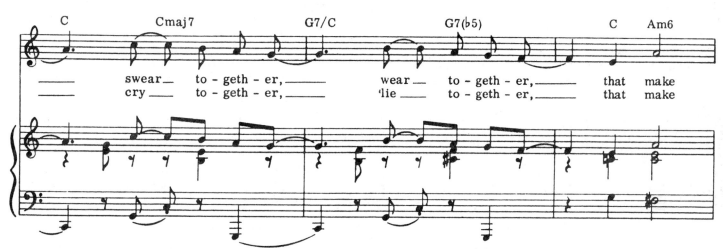

____ swear__ to - geth - er,____ wear__ to - geth - er,____ that make
____ cry__ to - geth - er,____ 'lie__ to - geth - er,____ that make

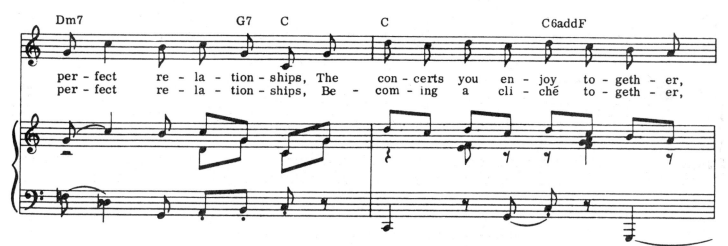

per - fect re - la - tion-ships, The con - certs you en - joy to - geth - er,
per - fect re - la - tion-ships, Be - com - ing a cli - ché to - geth - er,

140

LOSING MY MIND

from FOLLIES

Words and Music by
STEPHEN SONDHEIM

The sun comes up, I think about you. The cof-fee cup, I think a-bout

you. I want you so, It's like I'm los-ing my mind.

The morn-ing ends, I think a-bout you. I talk to friends, I think a-bout

142

LOST IN THE STARS
from the Musical Production LOST IN THE STARS

Words by MAXWELL ANDERSON
Music by KURT WEILL

long as the Lord God's watch-ing o-ver them, Keep-ing track how it all goes on. But I've been walk-ing through the night and the day Till my eyes get wear-y and my head turns gray, And some-times it seems may-be God's gone a-way, For-get-ting the prom-ise that we

MAKE SOMEONE HAPPY

from DO RE MI

Words by BETTY COMDEN and ADOLPH GREEN
Music by JULE STYNE

MAYBE
from the Musical Production ANNIE

Lyric by MARTIN CHARNIN
Music by CHARLES STROUSE

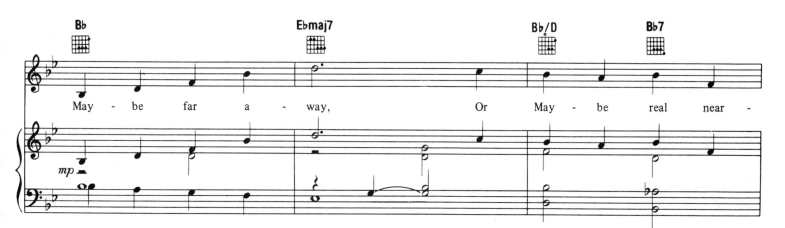

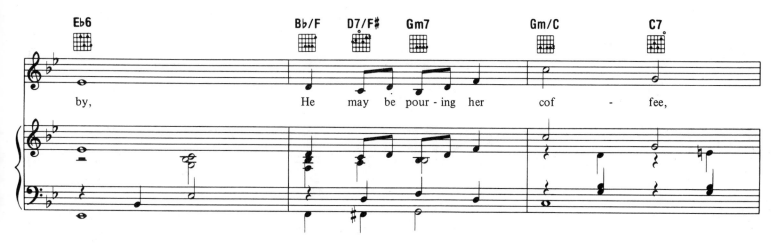

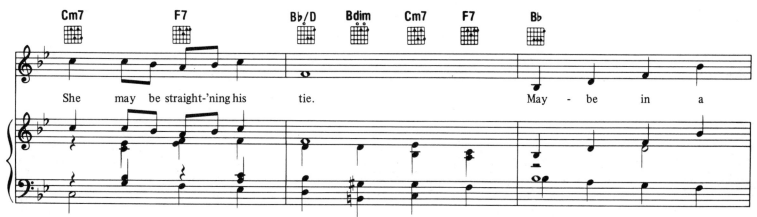

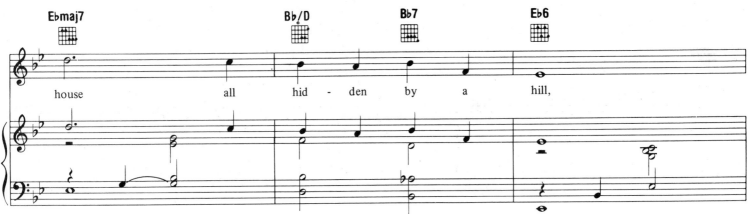

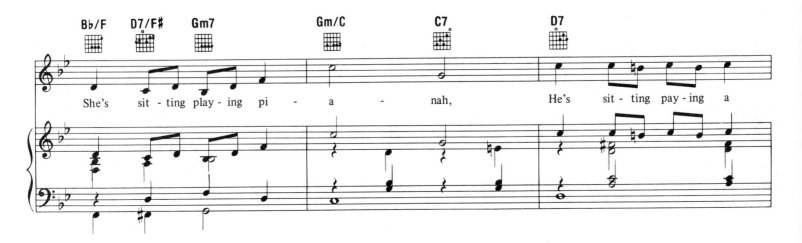

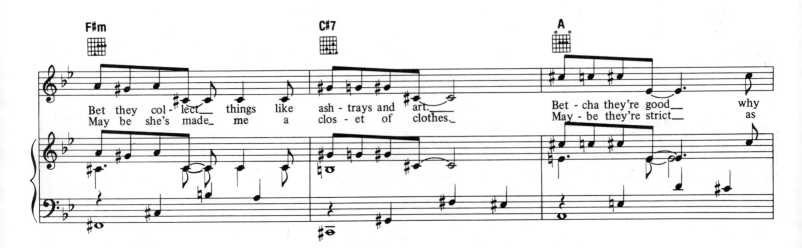

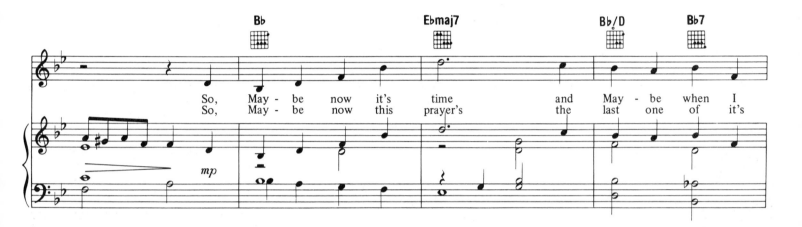

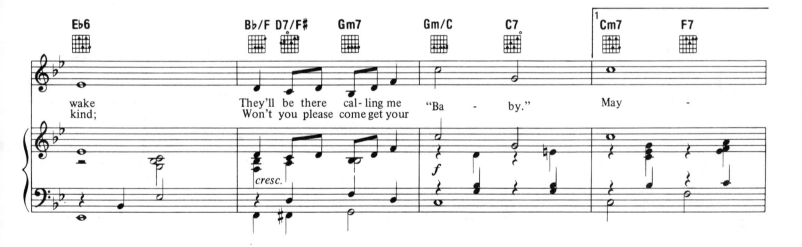

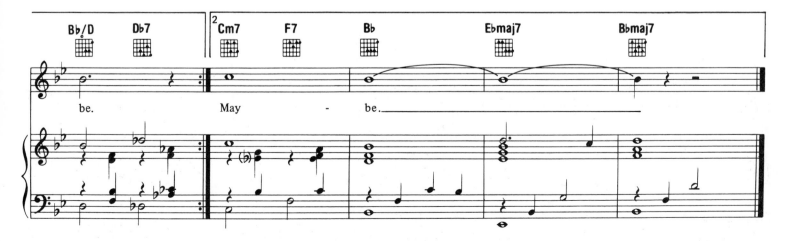

THE MUSIC OF THE NIGHT
from THE PHANTOM OF THE OPERA

Music by ANDREW LLOYD WEBBER
Lyrics by CHARLES HART
Additional Lyrics by RICHARD STILGOE

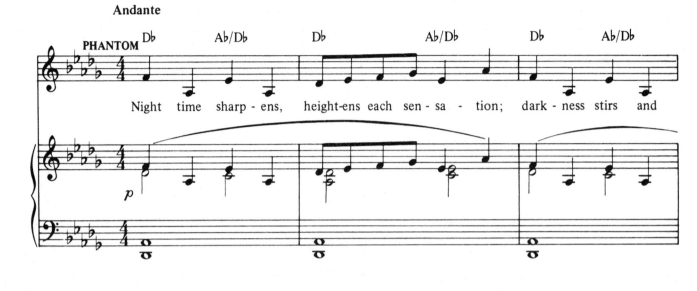

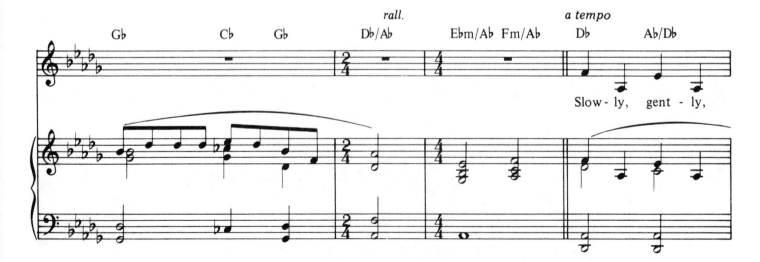

eyes let your spi-rit start to soar and you'll live as you've nev-er lived be - fore.

Soft - ly, deft - ly, mu - sic shall ca - ress you. Hear it, feel it,

se - cret-ly po - ssess you. O - pen up your mind let your fan - ta - sies un-wind in this

dark-ness which you know you can-not fight, the dark-ness of the mu-sic of the

157

night. Let your mind start a jour-ney through a strange, new world: leave all

thoughts of the world you knew be - fore. Let your soul take you where you long to

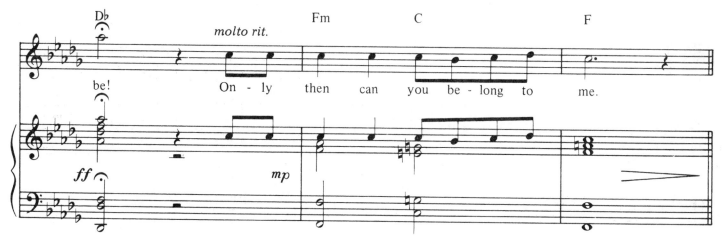

be! On - ly then can you be - long to me.

Float-ing, fall - ing, sweet in-tox-i - ca - tion. Touch me, trust me, sa-vour each sen-sa - tion.

A NEW LIFE
from JEKYLL & HYDE

Words by LESLIE BRICUSSE
Music by FRANK WILDHORN

Moderately slow, freely

with pedal

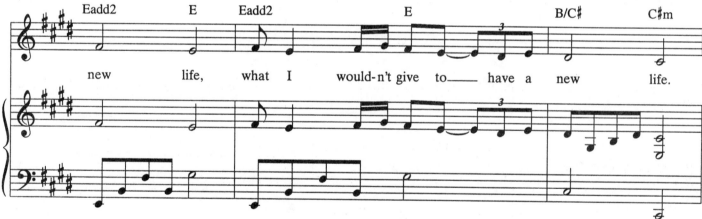

new life, what I would-n't give to___ have a new life.

One thing I have learned as I go through life,

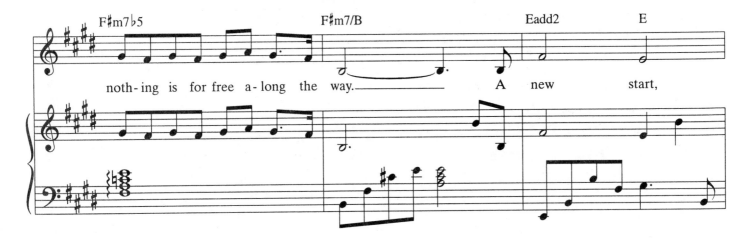

noth-ing is for free a-long the way._____ A new start,

that's the thing I need to give me new heart.

Half a chance in life_____ to find a new part,

just a sim-ple role that I can play._____ A new hope,

162

Moderately, in rhythm

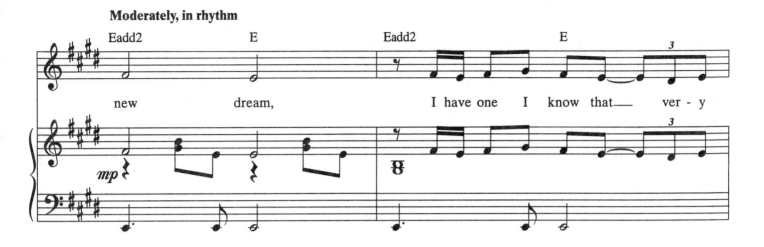

new dream, I have one I know that— ver - y

few dream. I would like to see that— o - ver -

due dream, e - ven though it nev - er may come

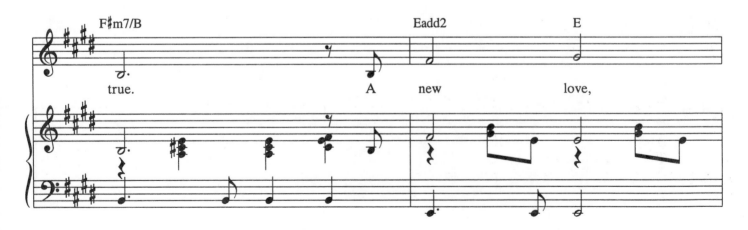

true. A new love,

163

though I know there's no such___ thing as true love.

E - ven so, al- though I_____ nev - er knew love,

still I feel that one dream___ is my due.

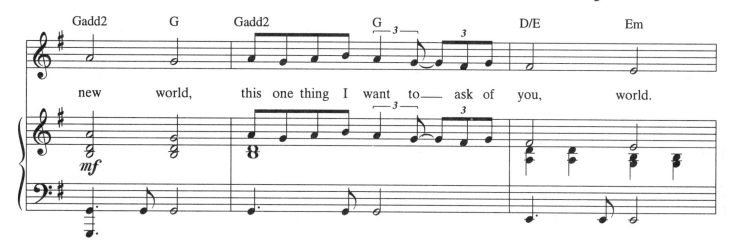

new world, this one thing I want to___ ask of you, world.

164

Once be - fore it's time to say a - dieu, world,

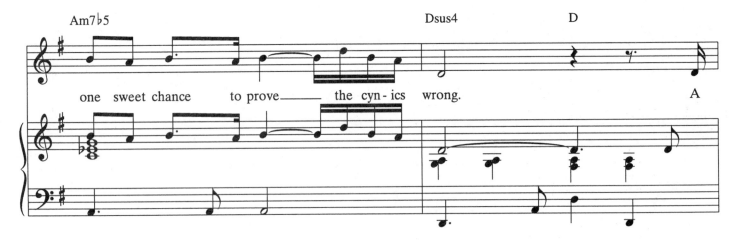

one sweet chance to prove the cyn - ics wrong.

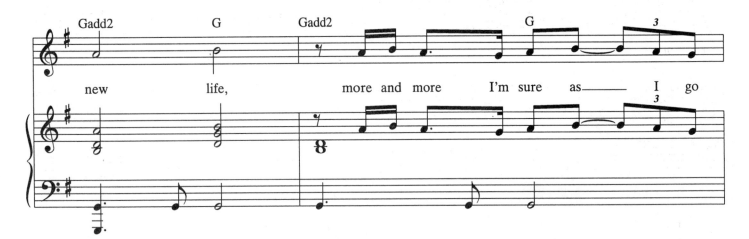

new life, more and more I'm sure as I go

through life. Just to play the game and to pur -

165

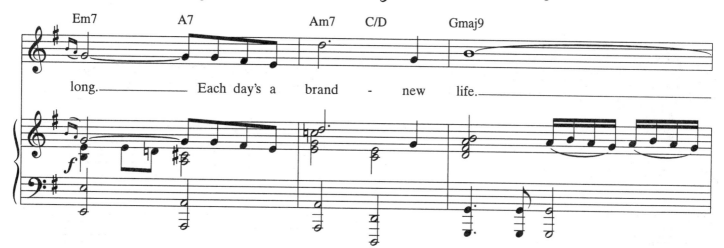

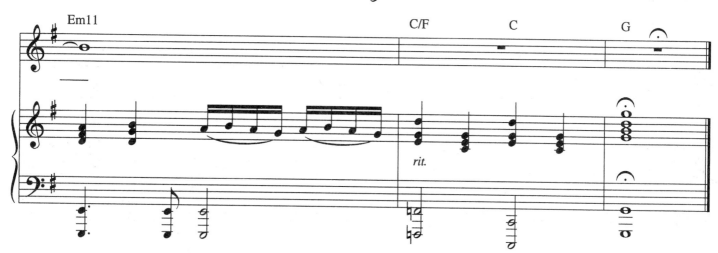

MY NEW PHILOSOPHY

from YOU'RE A GOOD MAN, CHARLIE BROWN

Words and Music by
ANDREW LIPPA

SALLY: *Spoken (before the vamp): "Why are you telling me?" (beat) I like it.*

* Original key: A Major
  The song is a duet for Sally and Schroeder. The composer created this solo edition for publication.

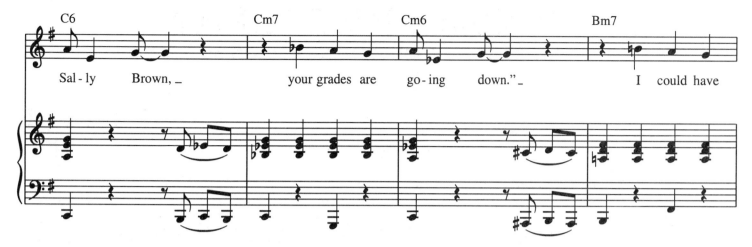

Sal - ly Brown, _ your grades are go - ing down." _ I could have

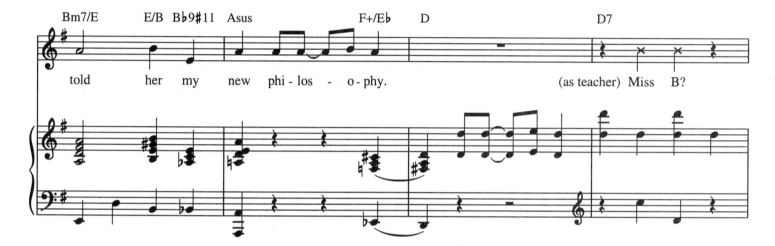

told her my new phi - los - o - phy. (as teacher) Miss B?

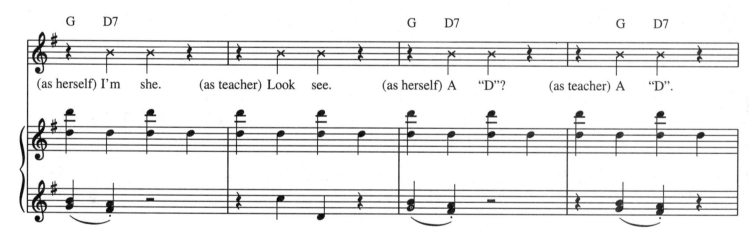

(as herself) I'm she. (as teacher) Look see. (as herself) A "D"? (as teacher) A "D".

Spoken (as herself): *Well, why are you telling me?* And that's my new phi - los - o - phy!! _

168

De-cid - ing _ what goes in it. Some take a life-time, mine take a

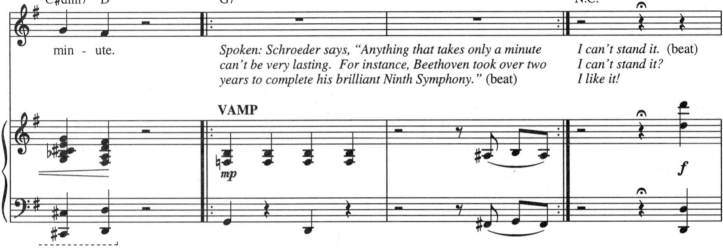

min - ute.

Spoken: Schroeder says, "Anything that takes only a minute can't be very lasting. For instance, Beethoven took over two years to complete his brilliant Ninth Symphony." (beat)

I can't stand it. (beat)
I can't stand it?
I like it!

Stride-time!

It's like a guar-an - tee, _ my new phi-los-o - phy, _

and things are sure to be _ a whole lot bright - er.

Spoken (trying out her new philosophies):
Oh yeah,

ON MY OWN
from LES MISÉRABLES

Music by CLAUDE-MICHEL SCHÖNBERG
Lyrics by ALAIN BOUBLIL, HERBERT KRETZMER, JOHN CAIRD,
TREVOR NUNN and JEAN-MARC NATEL

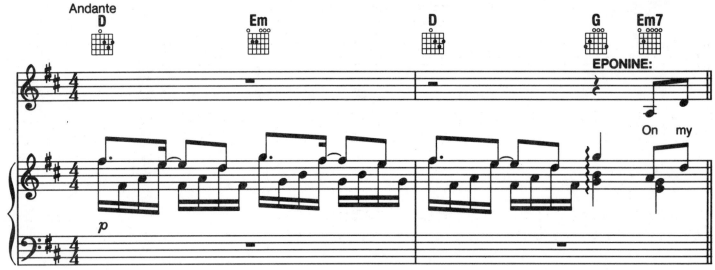

EPONINE:
On my

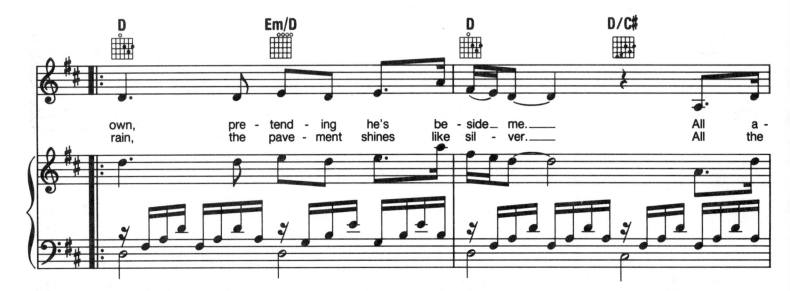

own, pre-tend-ing he's be-side me.___ All a-
rain, the pave-ment shines like sil-ver.___ All the

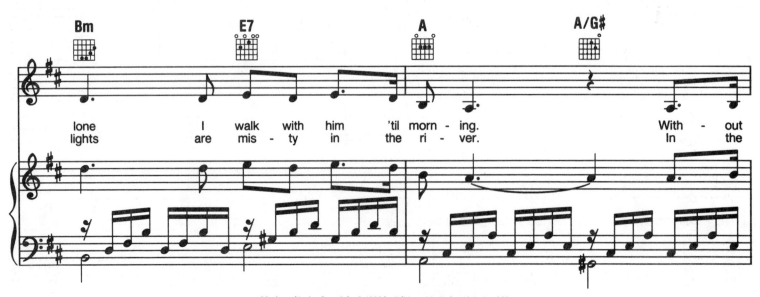

lone I walk with him 'til morn-ing. With-out the
lights are mis-ty in the ri-ver. In the

ONE
from A CHORUS LINE

Music by MARVIN HAMLISCH
Lyric by EDWARD KLEBAN

One smile and sud- den- ly no- bod- y

else will do, You know you'll

nev- er be lone- ly with you know who.

One mo- ment in her pres- ence

and you can for- get the rest,____

ONE MORE ANGEL IN HEAVEN

from JOSEPH AND THE AMAZING TECHNICOLOR® DREAMCOAT

Music by ANDREW LLOYD WEBBER
Lyrics by TIM RICE

mf BROTHERS

1 Fa - ther, we've some-thing to tell____ you, A sto - ry of our
2 Jo - seph____ died as he wished____ to,____ He an - swered du - ty's

think of his last____ great bat - tle,____ A lump comes to my

time. A tra - gic but in - spi - ring tale Of
call, He sin - gle - han - ded____ fought____ the beast That
throat. It____ takes a man who____ knows____ not fear to

man - hood in its____ prime.____ You know you had a____ do-
would have killed us____ all.____ His blood - stained coat is____ tri-
wres - tle with a____ goat.____ ALL BROTHERS Carve his name with pride

- zen sons, well now that's not quite true,____ But
- bute to his fi - nal sac - ri - fice,____ His
  and cour - age, let no tear be shed,____ If

182

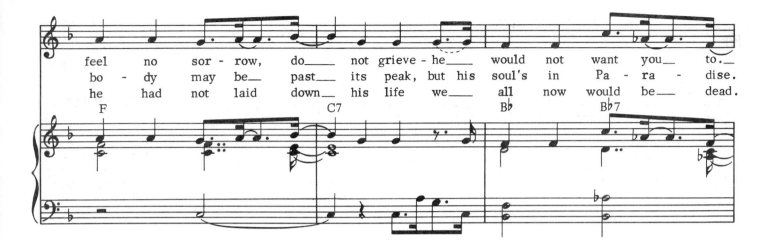

feel no sor - row, do___ not grieve - he___ would not want you___ to.___
bo - dy may be___ past___ its peak, but his soul's in Pa - ra - dise.
he had not laid down___ his life we___ all now would be___ dead.

F   C7   B♭   B♭7

There's one more an - gel in hea - ven,___ There's

Fm6   F   F   F

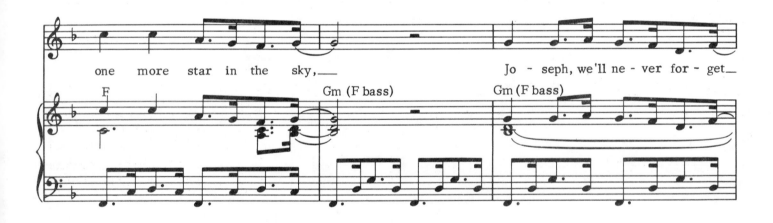

one more star in the sky,___ Jo - seph, we'll ne - ver for - get___

F   Gm (F bass)   Gm (F bass)

___ you,   It's tough but we're gon - na get by._____ There's

Gm (F bass)   C9   F

184

SEASONS OF LOVE

from RENT

Words and Music by
JONATHAN LARSON

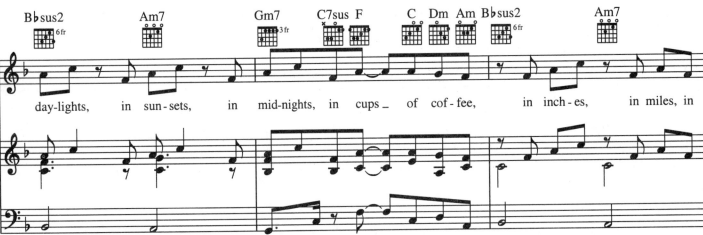

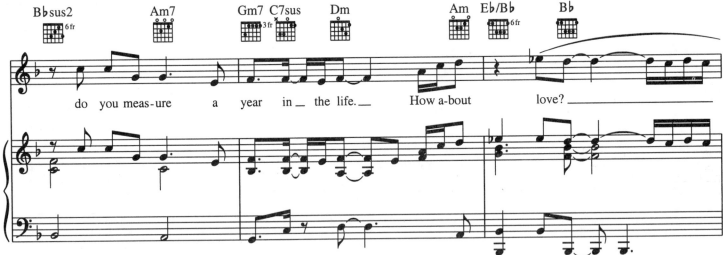

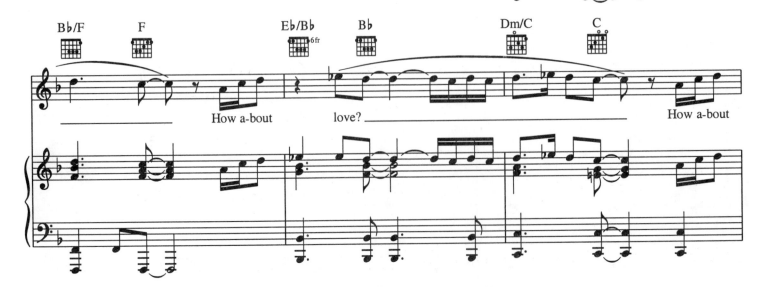

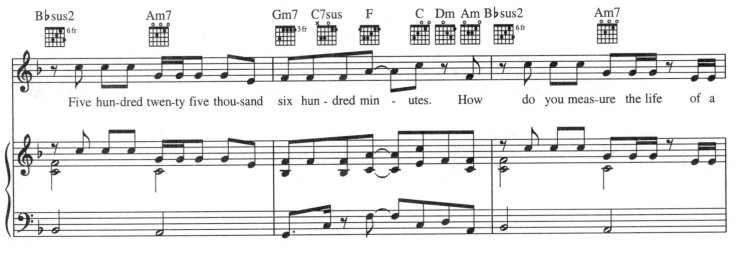

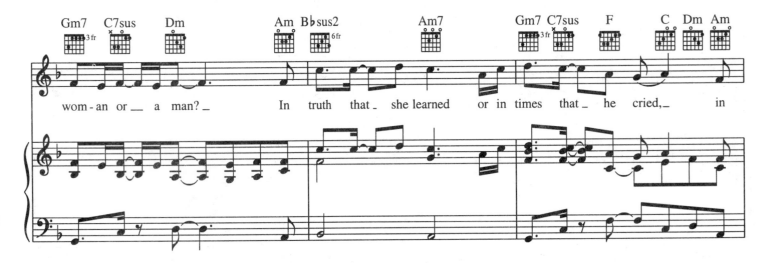

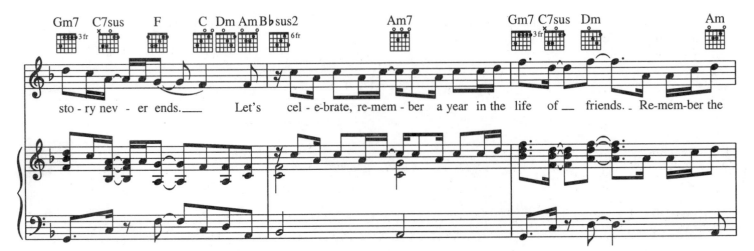

OUT OF MY DREAMS
from OKLAHOMA!

Lyrics by OSCAR HAMMERSTEIN II
Music by RICHARD RODGERS

SEPTEMBER SONG
from the Musical Play KNICKERBOCKER HOLIDAY

Words by MAXWELL ANDERSON
Music by KURT WEILL

SHADOWLAND

Disney Presents THE LION KING: THE BROADWAY MUSICAL

Music by HANS ZIMMER and LEBO M
Lyrics by MARK MANCINA and LEBO M

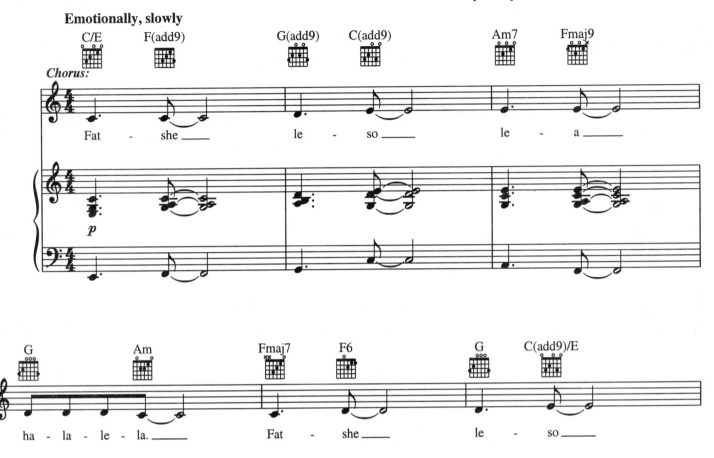

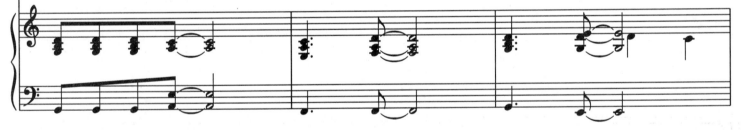

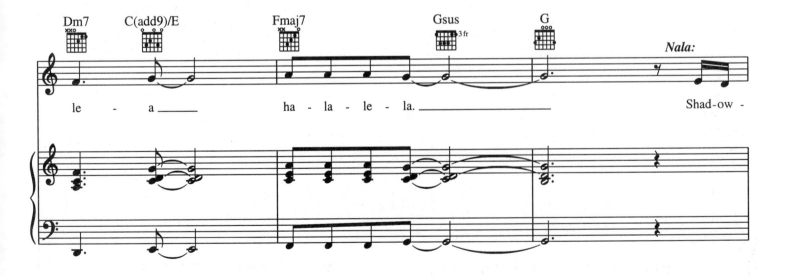

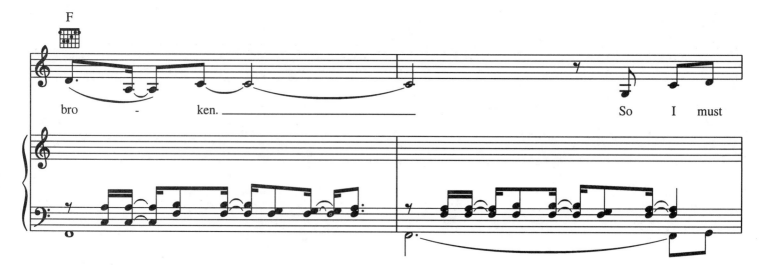

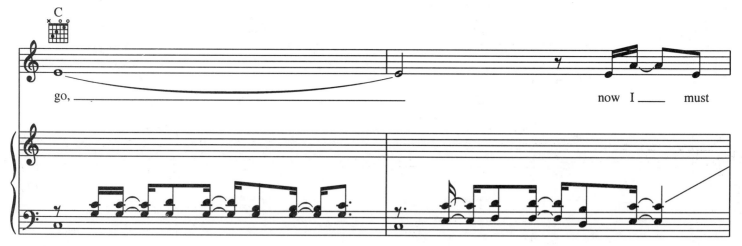

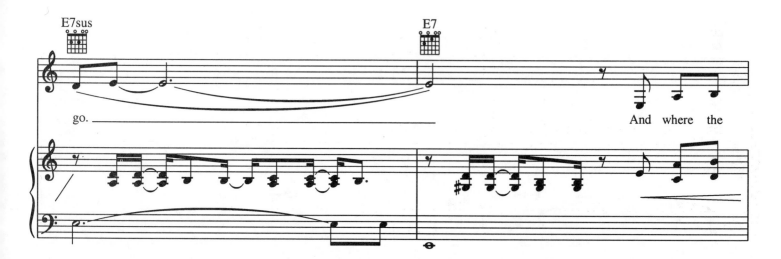

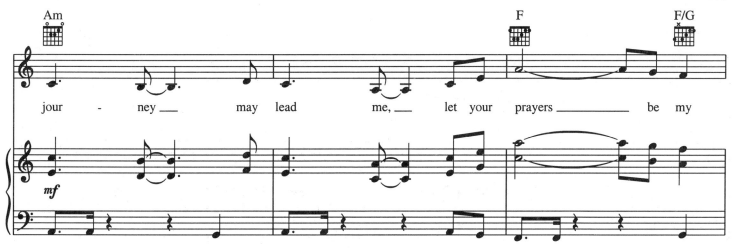

jour - ney ___ may lead me, ___ let your prayers ___ be my

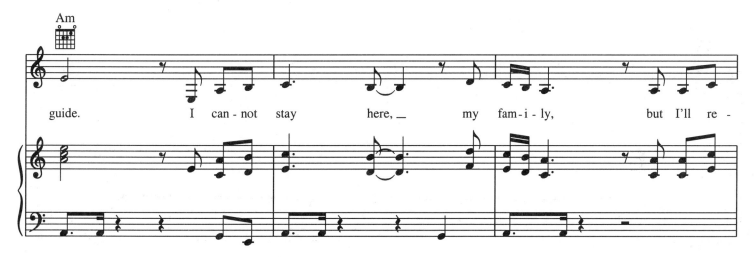

guide. I can - not stay here, ___ my fam-i-ly, but I'll re-

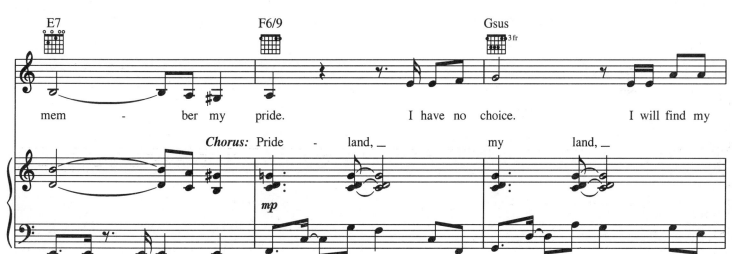

mem - ber my pride. I have no choice. I will find my

Chorus: Pride - land, ___ my land, ___

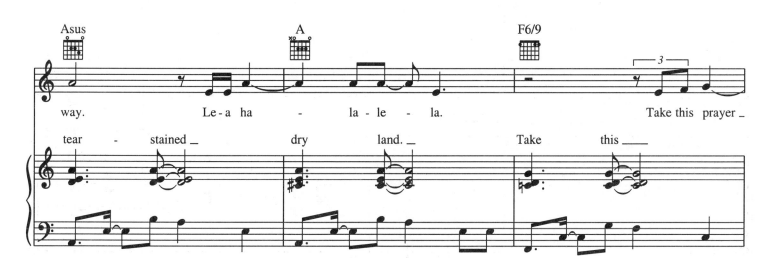

way. Le - a ha - la - le - la. Take this prayer ___

tear - stained ___ dry land. ___ Take this ___

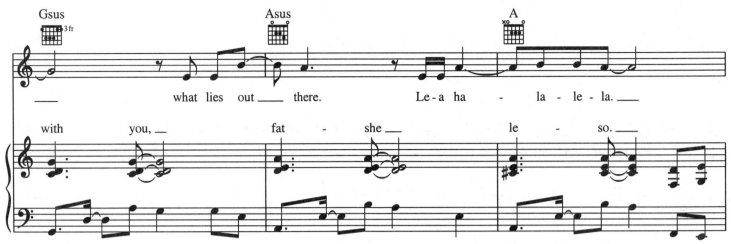

what lies out ____ there. Le - a ha - la - le - la. ____

with you, ____ fat - she ____ le - so. ____

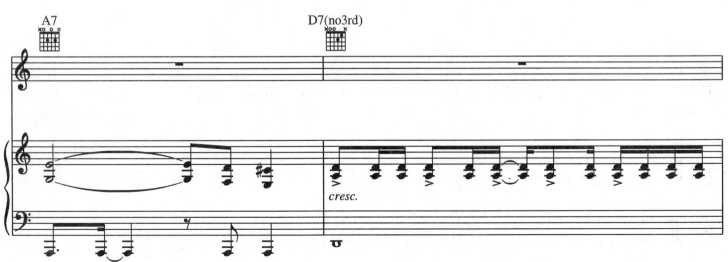

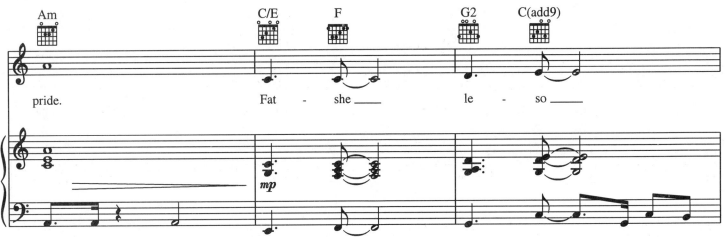

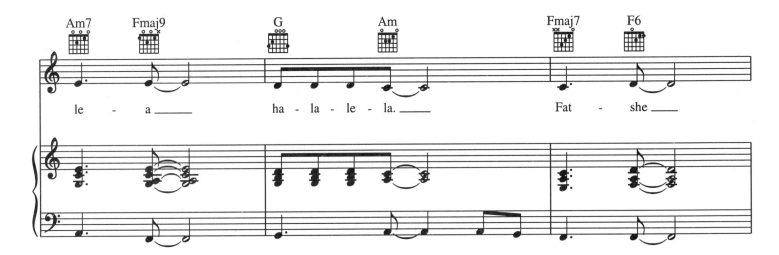

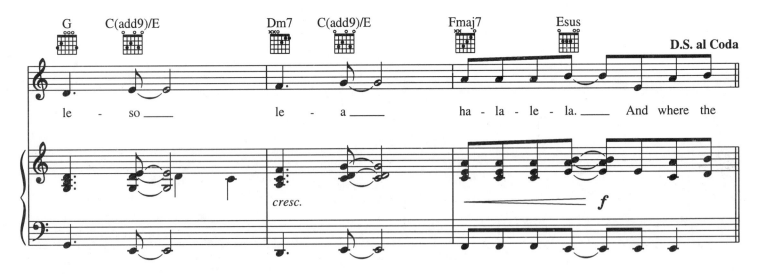

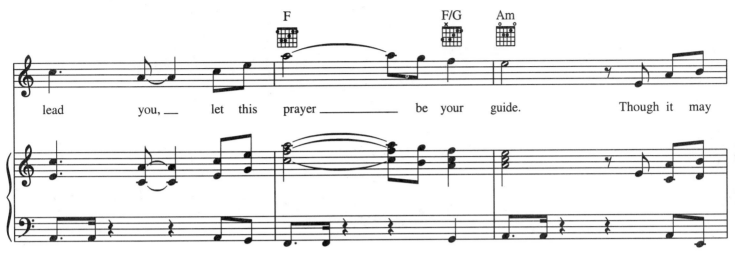

lead you, __ let this prayer __ be your guide. Though it may

take you __ so far-a-way, al-ways re-mem - ber your

pride. *(ad lib.)* **Nala:** Mm. __ Gi -

gi-za bu-ya-bo. __ Be - si-bo, __ my peo - ple, be-si-bo. __

SIT DOWN
YOU'RE ROCKIN' THE BOAT
from GUYS AND DOLLS

By FRANK LOESSER

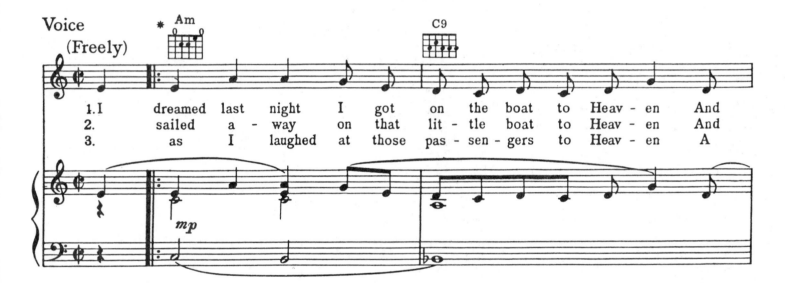

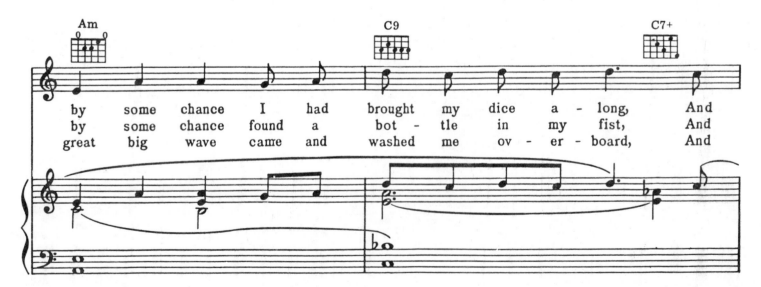

210

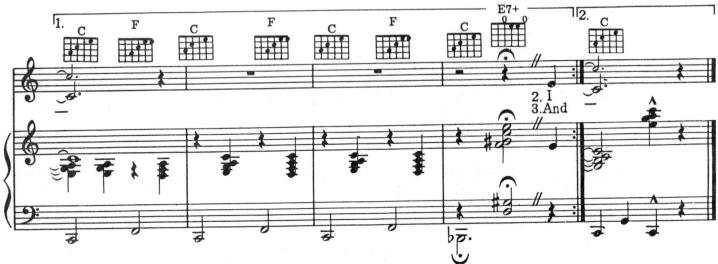

SOME ENCHANTED EVENING

from SOUTH PACIFIC

Lyrics by OSCAR HAMMERSTEIN II
Music by RICHARD RODGERS

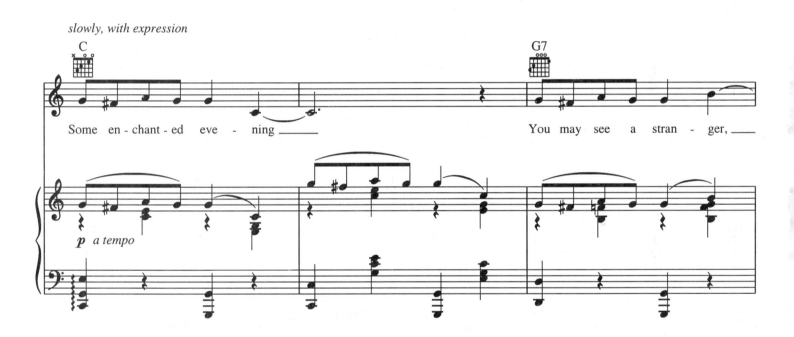

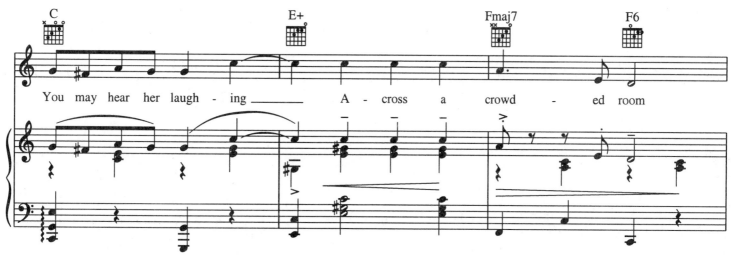

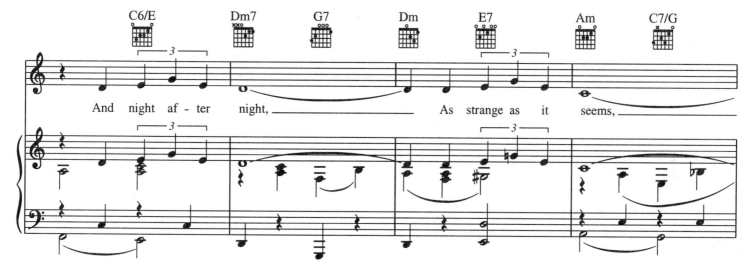

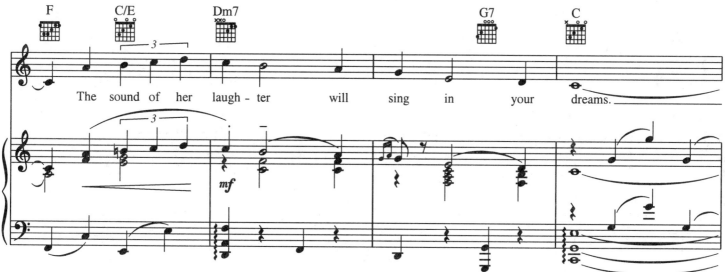

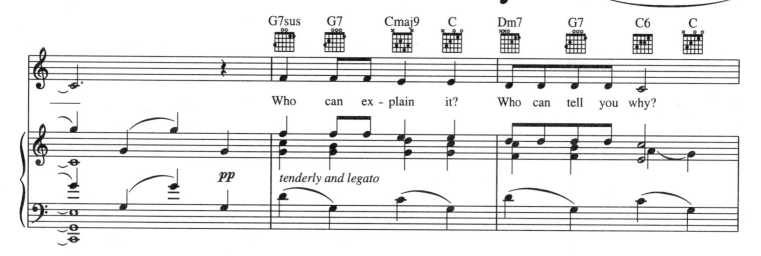

SOMEBODY, SOMEWHERE
from THE MOST HAPPY FELLA

By FRANK LOESSER

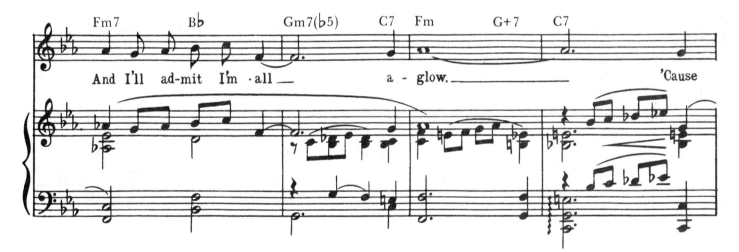

Wants lone-ly me to smile ___ and say hello ___ Some-bod-y, Some-where ___

wants me and needs me ___ And that's ver-y won-der-ful ___ to

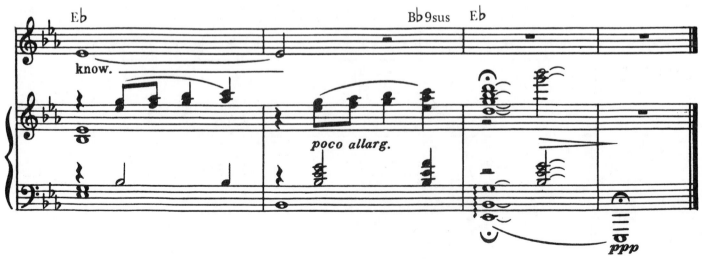

know.

SONG ON THE SAND
(La Da Da Da)
from LA CAGE AUX FOLLES

Music and Lyric by
JERRY HERMAN

Do you re-call that wind-y lit-tle beach we walked a-long? That af-ter-noon in fall, that af-ter-noon we met? A fel-la with a con-cer-ti-na sang; what was the song? It's strange what we re-call, and

SOMETHING WONDERFUL

from THE KING AND I

Lyrics by OSCAR HAMMERSTEIN II
Music by RICHARD RODGERS

SOPHISTICATED LADY
from SOPHISTICATED LADIES

Words and Music by DUKE ELLINGTON,
IRVING MILLS and MITCHELL PARISH

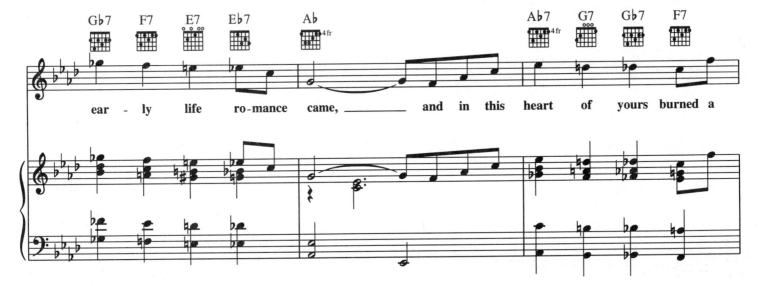

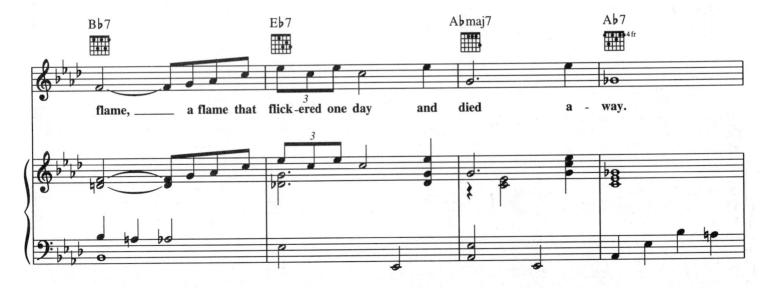

THE SURREY WITH THE FRINGE ON TOP

from OKLAHOMA!

Lyrics by OSCAR HAMMERSTEIN II
Music by RICHARD RODGERS

Brightly

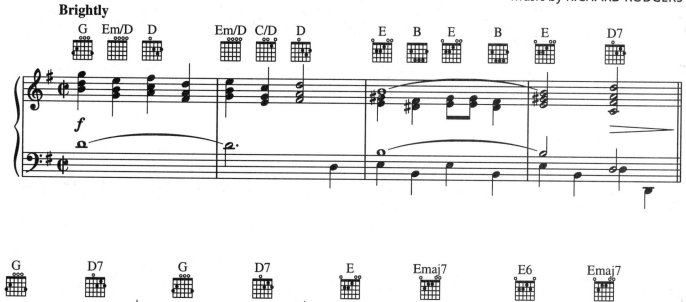

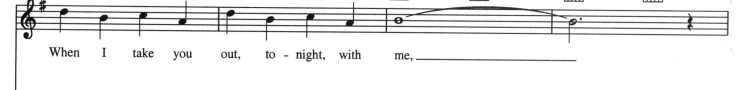

When I take you out, to-night, with me, _____

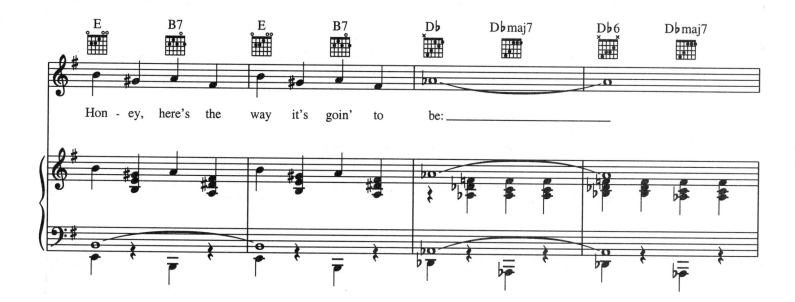

Hon-ey, here's the way it's goin' to be: _____

234

TELL ME ON A SUNDAY
from SONG AND DANCE

Music by ANDREW LLOYD WEBBER
Lyrics by DON BLACK

THEY CALL THE WIND MARIA
from PAINT YOUR WAGON

Words by ALAN JAY LERNER
Music by FREDERICK LOEWE

Lively

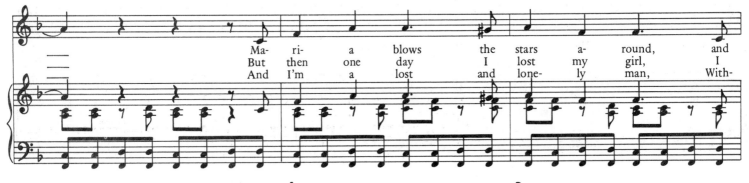

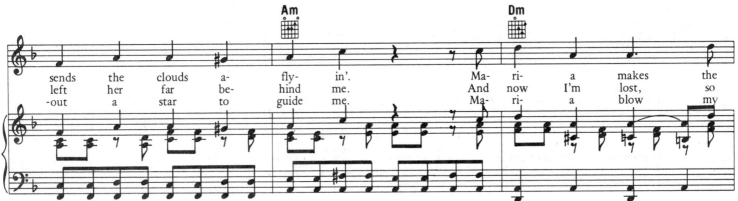

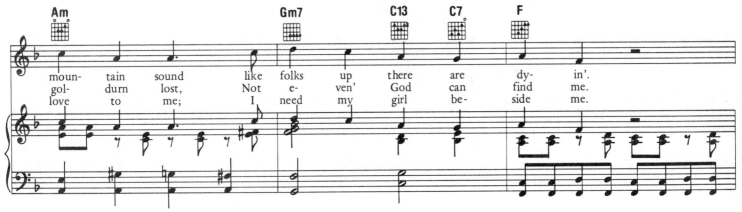

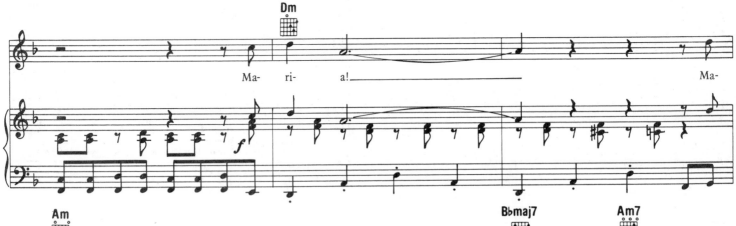

wind Ma- ri- a! Be-
Out

-ri- a! Ma- ri- a!

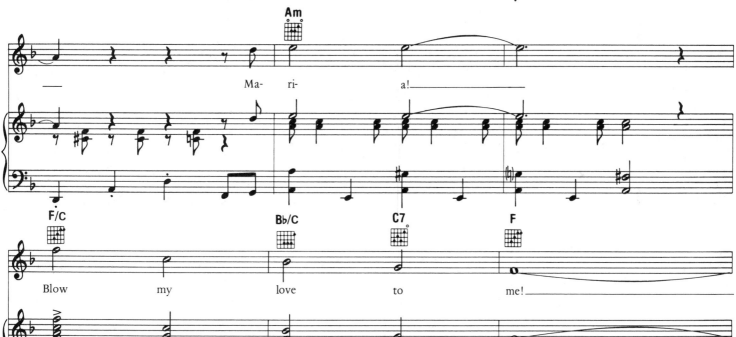

— Ma- ri- a!

Blow my love to me!

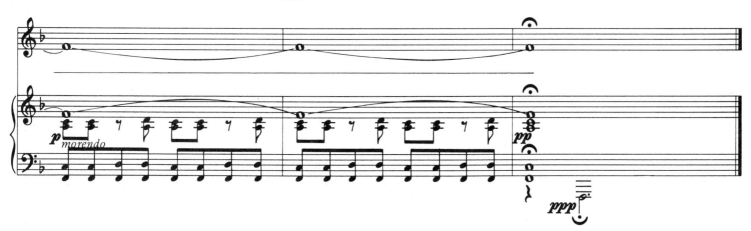

THERE'S NO BUSINESS LIKE SHOW BUSINESS

from the Stage Production ANNIE GET YOUR GUN

Words and Music by
IRVING BERLIN

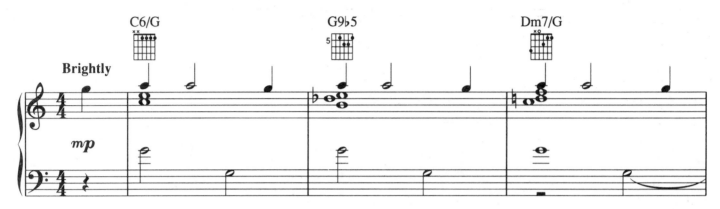

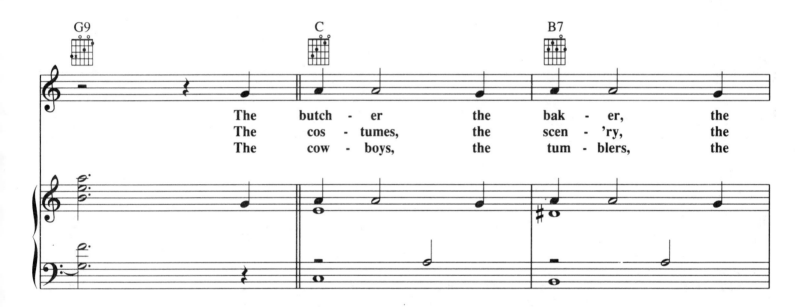

The butch - er the bak - er, the
The cos - tumes, the scen - 'ry, the
The cow - boys, the tum - blers, the

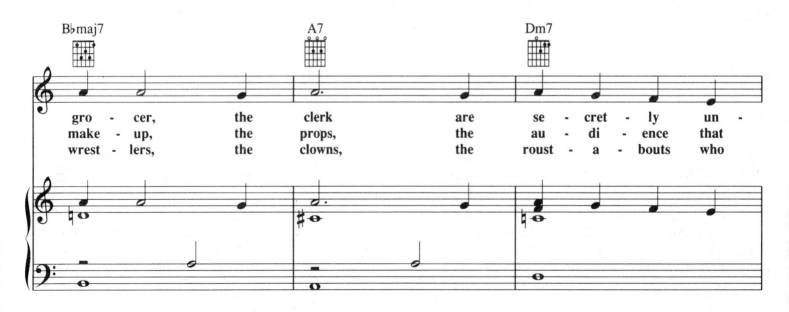

gro - cer, the clerk are se - cret - ly un -
make - up, the props, the au - di - ence that
wres - tlers, the clowns, the roust - a - bouts who

THEY DIDN'T BELIEVE ME
from THE GIRL FROM UTAH

Words by HERBERT REYNOLDS
Music by JEROME KERN

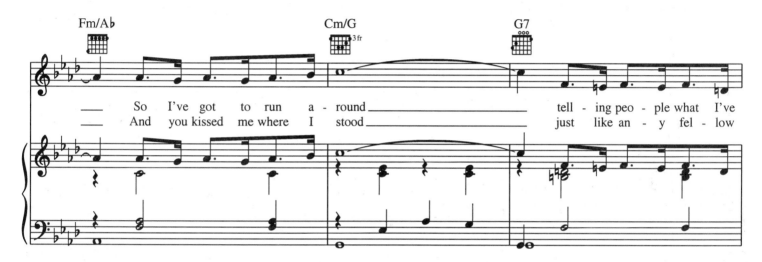

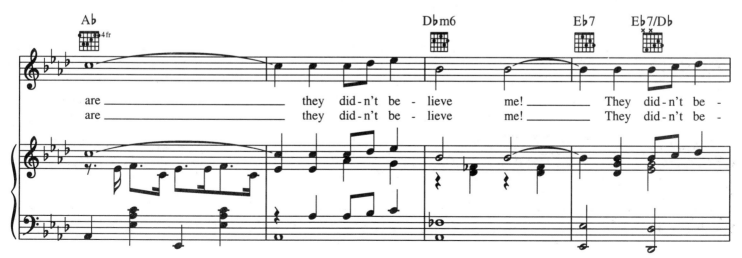

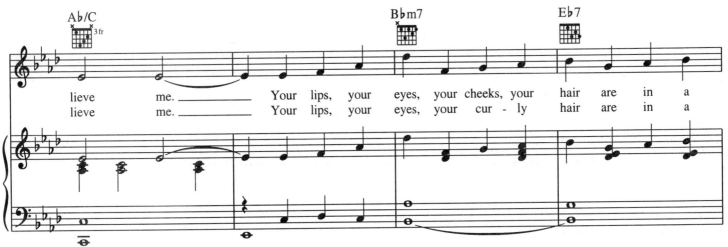

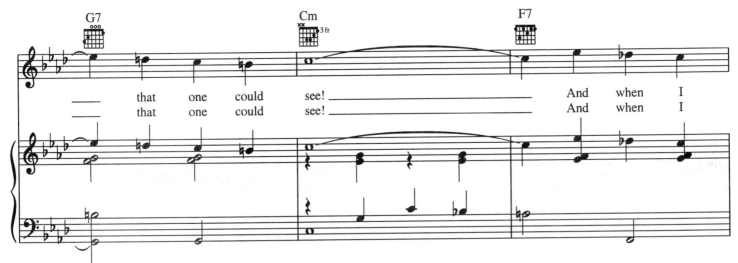

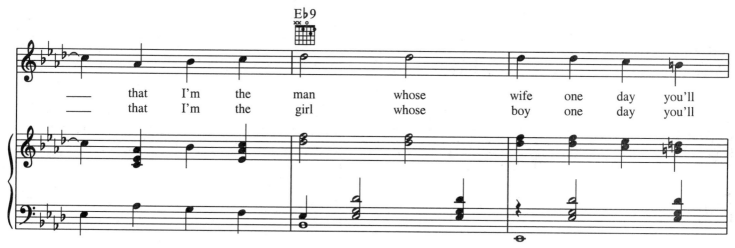

that I'm the man whose wife one day you'll
that I'm the girl whose boy one day you'll

be. _____ They'll nev - er be - lieve me, _____
be. _____ They'll nev - er be - lieve me, _____

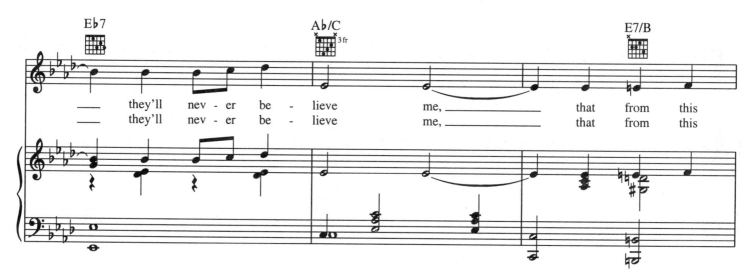

_____ they'll nev - er be - lieve me, _____ that from this
_____ they'll nev - er be - lieve me, _____ that from this

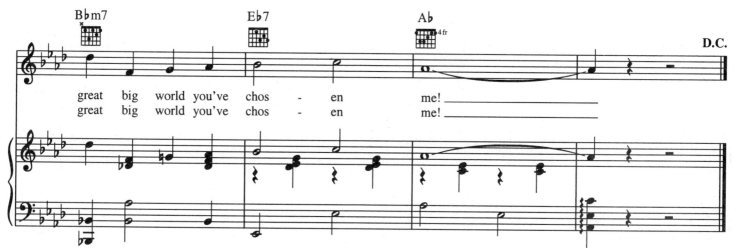

great big world you've chos - en me! _____
great big world you've chos - en me! _____

TOGETHER WHEREVER WE GO
from GYPSY

Words by STEPHEN SONDHEIM
Music by JULE STYNE

TURN BACK, O MAN
from the Musical GODSPELL

Words and Music by
STEPHEN SCHWARTZ

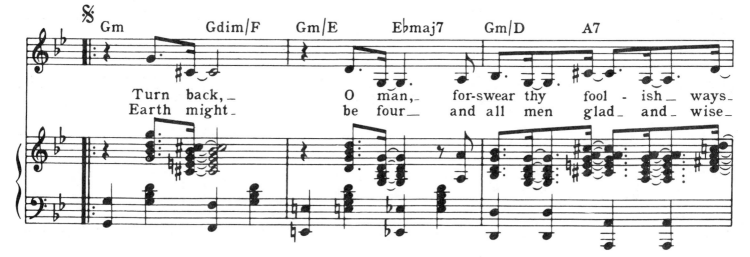

258

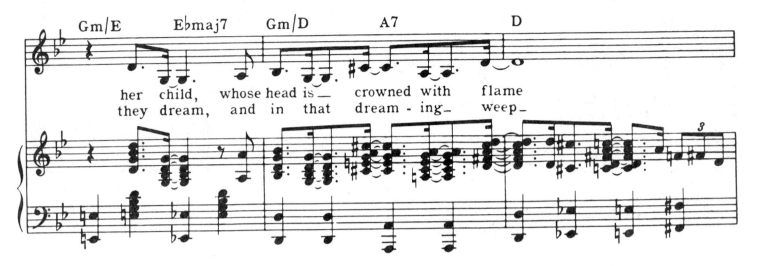

her child, whose head is — crowned with flame
they dream, and in that dream-ing— weep—

still walk not hear—————— thine in - ner— God— pro - claim

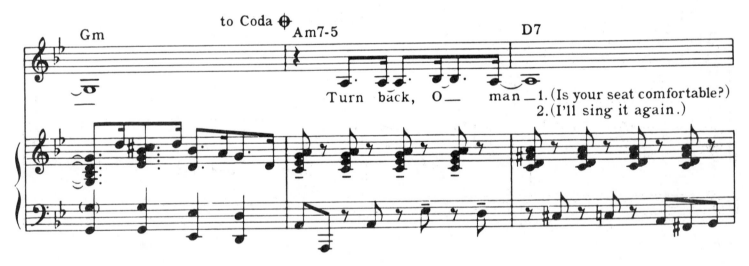

to Coda

Turn back, O— man— 1.(Is your seat comfortable?)
                      2.(I'll sing it again.)

Turn back, O— man—(Mmm I like that...)   Turn back, O— man—
(Can you see from where you're sittin'?)

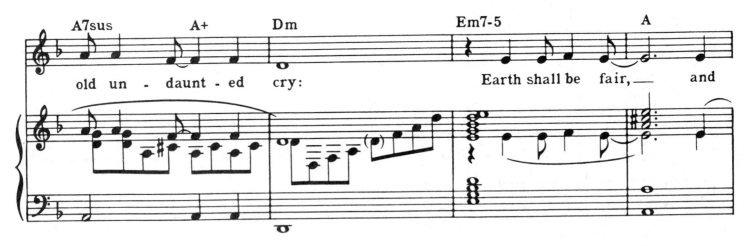

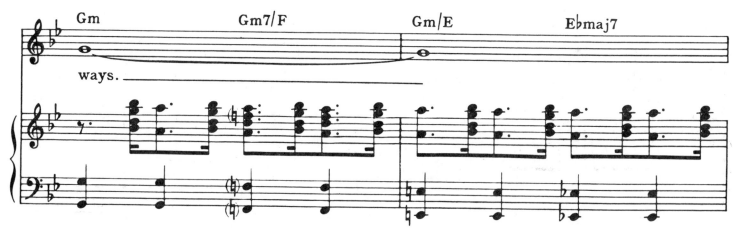

WHEN THE CHILDREN ARE ASLEEP

from CAROUSEL

Lyrics by OSCAR HAMMERSTEIN II
Music by RICHARD RODGERS

Refrain

WHO CAN I TURN TO

(When Nobody Needs Me)

from THE ROAR OF THE GREASEPAINT – THE SMELL OF THE CROWD

Words and Music by LESLIE BRICUSSE
and ANTHONY NEWLEY

Who can I turn to _____ when no-bo-dy needs me? My

heart wants to know and so I must go where des-ti-ny leads me. _____ With

no star to guide me, _____ and no- one be- side me, _____ I'll

WHO WILL LOVE ME AS I AM?

from SIDE SHOW

Words by BILL RUSSELL
Music by HENRY KRIEGER

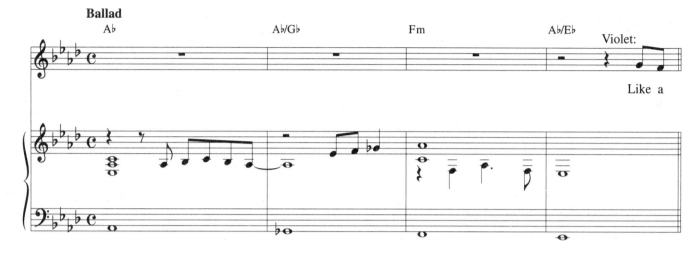

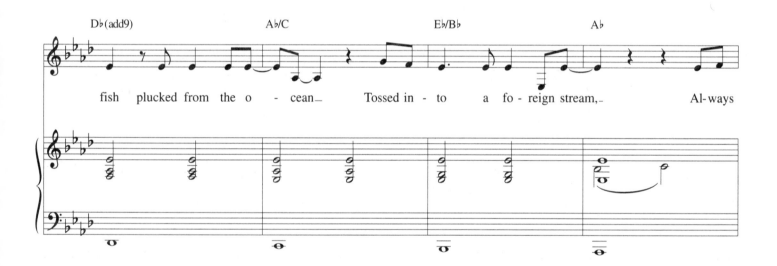

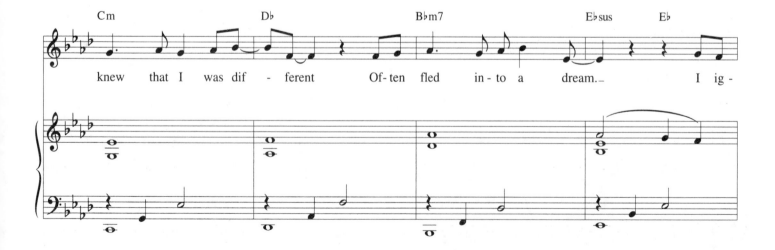

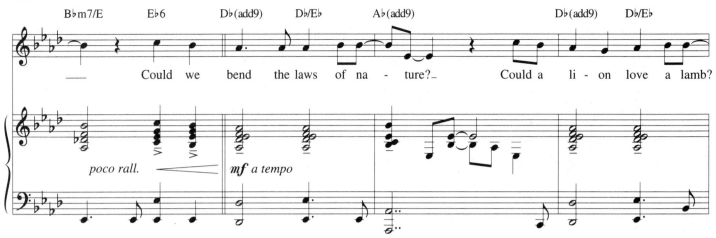

Bbm7/Eb — Eb6 — Db(add9) — Db/Eb — Ab(add9) — Db(add9) — Db/Eb

Could we bend the laws of na - ture?_ Could a li - on love a lamb?

poco rall. *mf a tempo*

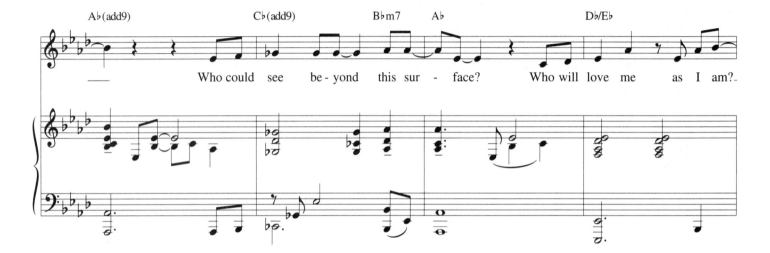

Ab(add9) — Cb(add9) — Bbm7 — Ab — Db/Eb

Who could see be - yond this sur - face? Who will love me as I am?_

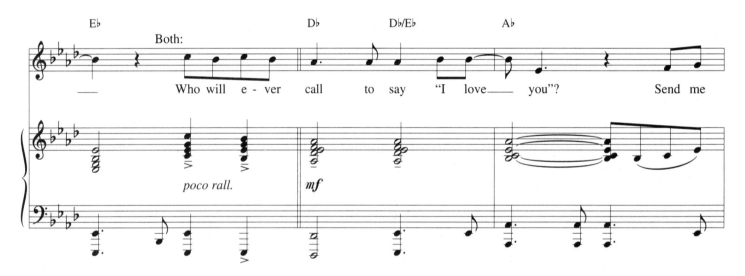

Eb — Db — Db/Eb — Ab

Both:

Who will e - ver call to say "I love____ you"? Send me

poco rall. *mf*

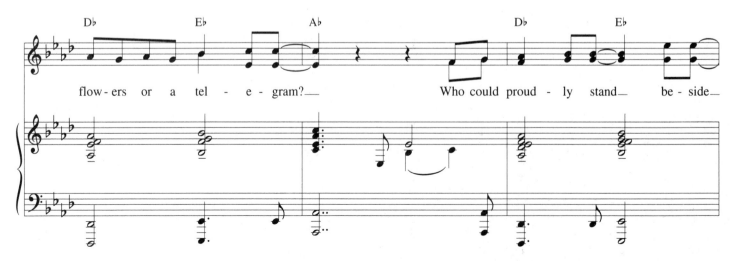

Db — Eb — Ab — Db — Eb

flow - ers or a tel - e - gram?_ Who could proud - ly stand_ be - side_

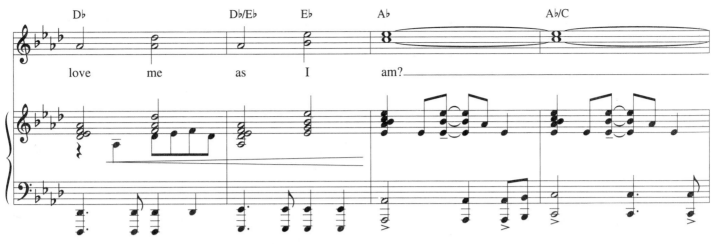

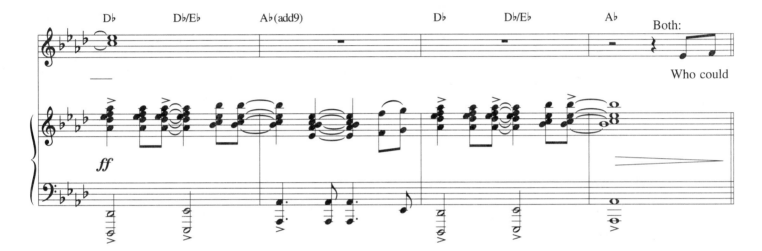

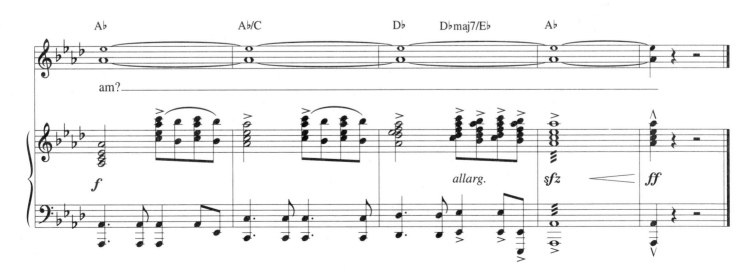

WILLKOMMEN
from the Musical CABARET

Words by FRED EBB
Music by JOHN KANDER

With spirit

G6/9

(Spoken
ad lib:) *Meine damen* Will - kom - men! *und* Bien - ve - *herren, Messieurs et* nue! *mes* Wel - come! *dames,* Ladies and

gentlemen, Frem - der, *Guten abend,* E - tran - ger, *Bon soir,*

275

WISHING YOU WERE SOMEHOW HERE AGAIN
from THE PHANTOM OF THE OPERA

Music by ANDREW LLOYD WEBBER
Lyrics by CHARLES HART
Additional Lyrics by RICHARD STILGOE

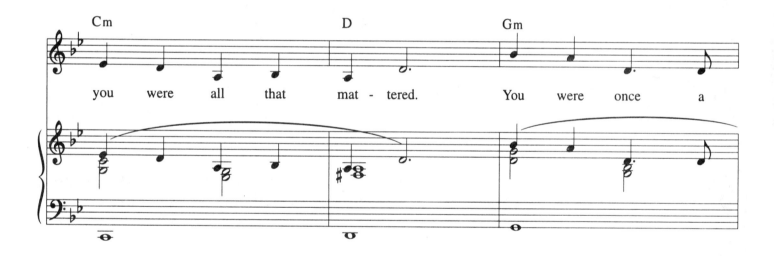

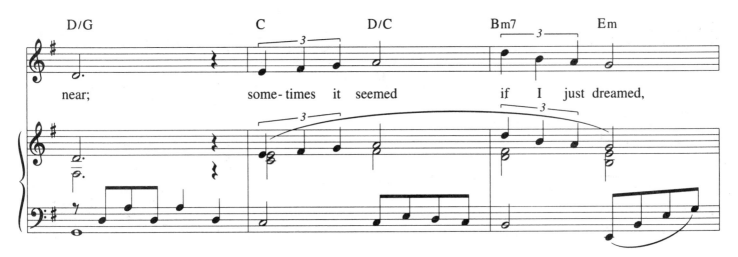

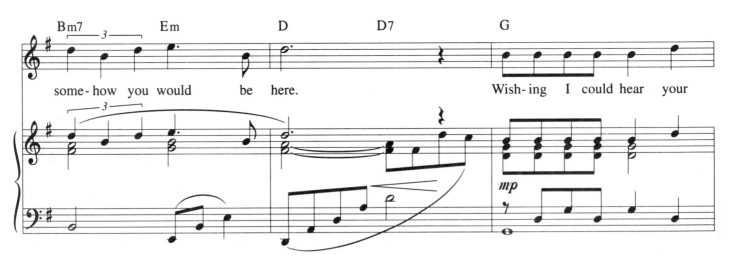

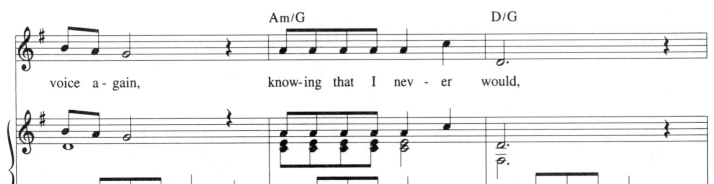

A WONDERFUL GUY

from SOUTH PACIFIC

Lyrics by OSCAR HAMMERSTEIN II
Music by RICHARD RODGERS

YOU DON'T KNOW THIS MAN

from PARADE

Music and Lyrics by
JASON ROBERT BROWN

Gm7   E♭maj7   Gm7

mf

mf   *a tempo*

you don't know this man.   I don't think you

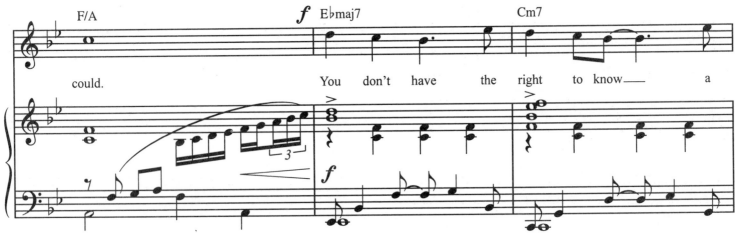

F/A   *f* E♭maj7   Cm7

could.   You don't have the right to know ____ a

f

E♭maj7   Cm6/D   D7♯5(♭9)   E♭maj7

man that wise and good. He is a de - cent man!

rall.

f   *a tempo*

Cm6   *mf*   E♭maj7   Cm6   *p*

He is an hon - est man!   And you don't

sub. *p*   *colla voce*   *mf* *a tempo*   *sub.* *p*

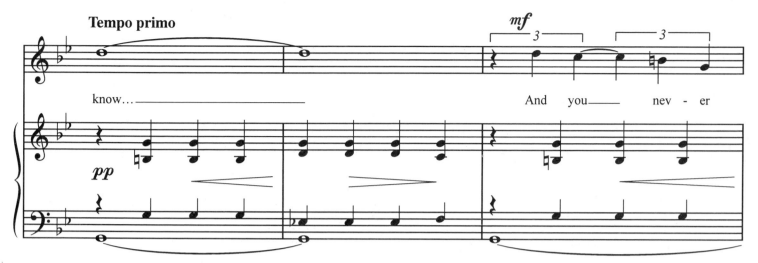

Tempo primo

mf

know... And you nev - er

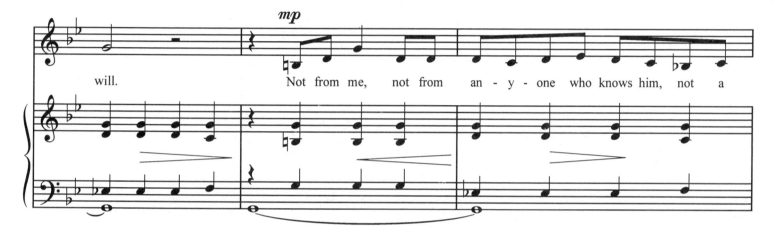

mp

will. Not from me, not from an - y - one who knows him, not a

Freely

mor - sel, not a crumb, not a clue. I have

poco rit.

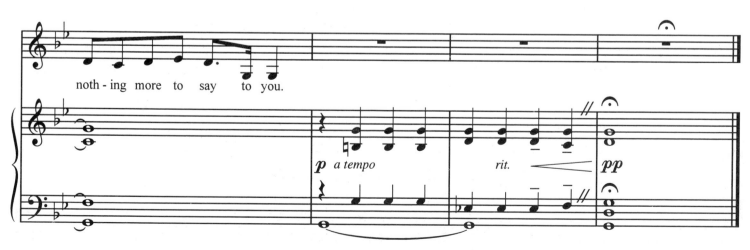

noth - ing more to say to you.

p a tempo *rit.*

YOU'RE A GOOD MAN, CHARLIE BROWN

from YOU'RE A GOOD MAN, CHARLIE BROWN

Words and Music by
CLARK GESNER

293

(I Wonder Why?)
YOU'RE JUST IN LOVE
from the Stage Production CALL ME MADAM

Words and Music by
IRVING BERLIN

298

Your heart goes pit - ter pat - ter. I know just

what's the mat - ter, be-cause I've been there once __ or twice. __

F   Gm7   Gb7b5   F

Put your head

on my shoul - der. You need some - one who's old - er.

THE TWENTIETH CENTURY SERIES

This beautiful series of songbooks celebrates the fir[st] century of recorded music and the many genres of music th[at] evolved over 100 years. Each book is arranged for piano an[d] voice with guitar chord frames.

THE 20TH CENTURY: BROADWAY

A comprehensive overview of 100 years of Broadway musicals with over 70 song[s] including: Ain't Misbehavin' • And All That Jazz • As If We Never Said Goodbye Beauty and the Beast • Brotherhood of Man • Cabaret • Close Every Door • Give [My] Regards to Broadway • Hello, Dolly! • I'd Give My Life for You • The Impossib[le] Dream (The Quest) • On My Own • One • Seasons of Love • Some Enchanted Eveni[ng] • Song on the Sand (La Da Da Da) • The Surrey with the Fringe on Top • and mor[e]

_____00310693 ....$19.9[5]

THE 20TH CENTURY: COUNTRY MUSIC

Over 70 country classics representative of a century's worth of music, including: All t[he] Gold in California • Always on My Mind • Amazed • Blue • Blue Eyes Crying in t[he] Rain • Blue Moon of Kentucky • Boot Scootin' Boogie • Breathe • Could I Have Th[is] Dance • Crazy • Folsom Prison Blues • Friends in Low Places • Harvey Valley P.T.[A.] • Hey, Good Lookin' • Jambalaya (On the Bayou) • King of the Road • Lucille • Rin[g] of Fire • Your Cheatin' Heart • and more.

_____00310673 ....$19.9[5]

THE 20TH CENTURY: JAZZ STANDARDS

Over 70 jazz standards that set the tone for the 20th century, including: All or Nothin[g] at All • Autumn in New York • Body and Soul • Brazil • Caravan • Don't Get Aroun[d] Much Anymore • Harlem Nocturne • How Deep Is the Ocean (How High Is the Sky[)] • I'm Beginning to See the Light • In the Mood • Manhattan • Misty • Route 66 • Satin Doll • Skylark • Slightly Out of Tune (Desafinado) • Star Dust • Stella b[y] Starlight • Take the "A" Train • and more!

_____00310696 ....$19.9[5]

THE 20TH CENTURY: LOVE SONGS

Over 60 of the century's favorite love songs, including: Always in My Heart (Siempr[e] en mi corazón) • And I Love Her • Cherish • (They Long to Be) Close to You • Jus[t] the Way You Are • Make It with You • (You Make Me Feel Like) A Natural Woman • Star Dust • Unexpected Song • The Very Thought of You • When I Fall in Love • Wonderful Tonight • You Are the Sunshine of My Life • You Needed Me • You've Go[t] a Friend • more.

_____00310698 ....$19.9[5]

THE 20TH CENTURY: MOVIE MUSIC

Over 60 of the century's best songs from the cinema, including: Be a Clown • Chang[e] the World • Chariots of Fire • Do You Know Where You're Going To? • Endless Lov[e] • Footloose • Hakuna Matata • I Will Remember You • Love Story • Moon River • My Heart Will Go On (Love Theme from 'Titanic') • Supercalifragilisticexpialidociou[s] • Tears in Heaven • Unchained Melody • The Way We Were • more.

_____00310694 ....$19.9[5]

THE 20TH CENTURY: THE ROCK ERA

Over 60 songs that defined the rock era, including: Baby Love • Bohemian Rhapsod[y] • Dancing in the Street • Dust in the Wind • Eleanor Rigby • Fire and Rain • Heartbreak Hotel • I Got You (I Feel Good) • Imagine • Layla • Oh, Pretty Woman • Piano Man • Surfin' U.S.A. • Time After Time • Twist and Shout • Wild Thing • mor[e]

_____00310697 ....$19.9[5]

FOR MORE INFORMATION, SEE YOUR LOCAL MUSIC DEALER, OR WRITE TO:

HAL•LEONARD®
CORPORATION

7777 W. BLUEMOUND RD. P.O. BOX 13819 MILWAUKEE, WI 53213

Visit Hal Leonard Online at
www.halleonard.com

MAR 2002

Prices, contents, and availability subject to change without notice.